THE WORK OF

JOHN VANBRUGH

W0006080

SIR JOHN VANBRUGH 1664-1726. Painting by Sir Godfrey Kneller, oil on canvas, 91.4 × 71.1 cm (36 × 28 in), *c* 1704-10, s. in monogram, National Portrait Gallery, London, No. 3231 (Photograph: Gallery).

THE WORK OF

JOHN VANBRUGH

Geoffrey Beard

illustrated by
Anthony Kersting

B. T. BATSFORD LTD
LONDON

© GEOFFREY BEARD AND ANTHONY KERSTING 1986
FIRST PUBLISHED 1986

ALL RIGHTS RESERVED. NO PART OF THIS PUBLICATION
MAY BE REPRODUCED, IN ANY FORM OR BY ANY MEANS,
WITHOUT PERMISSION FROM THE PUBLISHERS

ISBN 0 7134 4678 1 (cased)
0 7134 4679 X (limp)

TYPESET AND PRINTED IN ENGLAND
BY BUTLER & TANNER LTD, FROME AND LONDON
FOR THE PUBLISHER
B. T. BATSFORD LTD,
4 FITZHARDING STREET, LONDON W1H 0AH

CONTENTS

TO THE READER

In this prefatory note I want to say a little about the extent of this short book on Vanbrugh, and explain why it was undertaken. In 1978, and again in 1982, I collaborated with the architectural photographer, Anthony Kersting, in providing two books on the work of Robert Adam, and of Christopher Wren. The array of high-quality illustrations, coupled with a short text, and notes on the plates incorporating relevant research, ensured them considerable success. *The Work of Robert Adam* is now in its third impression, and has spawned a shorter study on his country houses. We were asked to repeat the process for perhaps the most exciting architect England reared: Sir John Vanbrugh.

The text of this book is intended to be concise; it selects essentials, and directs readers who wish to know a great deal more about Vanbrugh to specialist articles and longer books. However, we consider our illustration coverage to be above average. In thinking about Vanbrugh I was fortunate that my friends included the five scholars who had contributed most to an understanding of his complex personality – the late Professor Geoffrey Webb, who edited Vanbrugh's *Letters*, and told very good stories about doing so; Laurence Whistler, who spent many years considering Vanbrugh, writing books about his work in 1938 and 1954; David Green, the historian of Blenheim Palace, of Sarah, Duchess of Marlborough, and of the Churchills; Howard Colvin, author of the standard biographical dictionary about British architects, and editor of *The History of the King's Works*; and Professor Kerry Downes, whose two seminal volumes on Hawksmoor are equalled only by his important study of Vanbrugh (1977). Each helped by enthusiastic support – Professor Webb and Howard Colvin at an early point in developing my interests in architectural history – and by suggestions for research ranging from the basic one to write the book (Howard Colvin), to the loan or location of photographs difficult to obtain. They were and are absolved from any responsibility for the ways I have used their information, but as Vanbrugh had it, on 25 December 1718: 'I did my best to make the most on't.'

I am much indebted to the owners of Vanbrugh houses or memorabilia, all of whom provided information and allowed us to take photographs. This is applicable in particular to the Duke of Marlborough, and to the late Lord Howard of Henderskelfe, because we were at their 'great, fine houses' the longest. I regret that Lord Howard, who had gone out of his way to aid our work for over 30 years – Mr Kersting and I first went together to Castle Howard in 1954 – did not live to see this short study completed. Simon Howard encouraged us to continue at a difficult time for him.

For further help of various kinds warm thanks are due to: Geoffrey de Bellaigue, Eileen Carvell, Revd Edward Corbould O.S.B., Paul Duffie, R. M. Gard, Dr Eric Gee, Sir Nicholas and Lady Goodison, P. B. Grimes, Hardwick Holderness, Mr and Mrs E. Lamb, Lord Montagu of Beaulieu, Sir Oliver Millar, Revd Dominic Milroy O.S.B., Lord and Lady Mowbray and Stourton, William Proby, the Hon. James Stourton, Sir John Summerson, Dr Nigel Whiteley, Dr Peter Willis, and Colin Wilson. At a crucial point John Harris discussed certain problems, and provided helpful advice which led to the location of the family Bible (pl. 2). Dr Terry Friedman shared information obtained in his own researches on James Gibbs. The staffs of the Birmingham Reference Library (particularly Philip Allen), Bristol University Library, the Courtauld Institute, and the National Monuments Record (particularly Stephen Croad) provided photographs and books for publication, or research.

Finally 'the author in his own home' was humoured, often as a detached 'third person', by his wife Margaret. Tim Auger, as publisher, remained cheerful at the usual delays in waiting for the right weather for photography and in completing the book. The last words to the reader should be those of Vanbrugh, on April 19, 1716:

> I hope the offering these things to your ... thoughts may rather prove some small amusement than a trouble to you, tis at least on that account this comes from
> You ever obedient and Most faithfully servant ...

Bath,   *Geoffrey Beard*
May 1986.

ILLUSTRATION
ACKNOWLEDGEMENTS

All the photographs were specially taken for this book by Anthony Kersting, with the exception of the following for which we give grateful acknowledgement:

Birmingham Reference Library; 8, 19, 39, 40, 41, 45, 54, 57, 70, 71, 72, 74, 75, 90, 106, 107, 113, 114, 115; Bodleian Library; 53, 61; British Library; 38; Cambridge University; 30; A. C. Cooper; 125; Courtauld Institute of Art; 4, 20, 21, 22, 23, 44, 59, 65, 66, 68, 84, 92, 93, 94, 99, 112; Metropolitan Museum of Art, New York; 103; National Monuments Record; 33, 86, 105; National Portrait Gallery; 1, 7; Palace House, Beaulieu; 36; R.I.B.A.; 15; Sir John Soane's Museum; 3; University of York; 5; Victoria and Albert Museum; 9, 10, 16, 17, 24, 69, 73, 80, 95, 96, 97; Laurence Whistler; 123, 124.

ABBREVIATIONS

Colvin, *Dictionary*	H. M. Colvin, *A Biographical Dictionary of British Architects, 1600–1840* (1978)
Colvin, *King's Works, V.*	H. M. Colvin, ed., *The History of the King's Works, V, 1660–1782* (1976)
Colvin and Craig	H. M. Colvin and M. Craig, *Architectural Drawings in the Library of Elton Hall by Sir John Vanbrugh and Sir Edward Lovett Pearce*, Oxford, for the Roxburghe Club (1964)
Croft-Murray, I or II	Edward Croft-Murray, *Decorative Painting in England, 1530–1837*, 2 vols., I (1962), II (1970)
Dobrée, *Works*	Bonamy Dobrée, ed., *The Complete Works of Sir John Vanbrugh*, 4 vols (1927–8), (see Webb, below)
Downes	Kerry Downes, *Vanbrugh* (1977)
Green, *Blenheim*	David Green, *Blenheim Palace* (1951)
Green, *Sarah, Duchess*	David Green, *Sarah, Duchess of Marlborough* (1967)
Tipping and Hussey	H. A. Tipping and Christopher Hussey, *English Homes IV. 2. The Work of Sir John Vanbrugh and his School, 1699–1736* (1928)
Webb, *Letters*	Geoffrey Webb, ed., *The Complete Works of Sir John Vanbrugh*, Vol. IV, *The Letters* (1928)
Whistler, 1938	Laurence Whistler, *Sir John Vanbrugh: Architect and Dramatist* (1938)
Whistler	Laurence Whistler, *The Imagination of Vanbrugh and his Fellow Artists* (1954)
Wren Soc.	A. T. Bolton and H. D. Hendry, eds., *The Wren Society*, vols. I–XX (1924–43) – cumulative index, vol. XX

CW01024445

I

A Man of Wit, and of Honour

In regard to Two Persons only we wish our Railery, though ever so tender, or Resentment, though ever so just, had not been indulged. We speak of Sir John Vanbrugh, who was a Man of Wit, and of Honour, and of Mr Addison....

Jonathan Swift and Alexander Pope, joint Preface to Swift's *Miscellanies in Prose*, 1727

In 1714, the year of George I's accession following the death of Queen Anne, Vanbrugh, who had held office in the College of Arms since 1703, thought it expedient to obtain confirmation of his arms. He had reason to believe it would be recalled that in 1706 at Hanover he had waited on the future King, Georg August, then Elector of Brunswick, to deliver the Order of the Garter. This was in the company of Lord Halifax, and, significantly, Swift's other nominee for late favour, Joseph Addison. He was Under Secretary of State, but in addition a seminal influence on Vanbrugh's development as a gardener and on English gardening theory. Vanbrugh let a house to him in later years in Kensington and subscribed to his published *Works*. He had joined him in 1706 in Amsterdam.[1] Would the carrying of the Garter be reason enough for preferment and royal favour? What he was soon to learn, with excitement, was that the day after the King landed at Greenwich, 19 September 1714, he was to be dubbed as the first knight of the new reign. He would not realize for some time, that the act had more to do with the intervention of his patron at Blenheim, the 1st Duke of Marlborough, newly returned to high position. Vanbrugh had but four further months to wait until the Comptrollership to the Board of Works was also restored to him.

In support of the application about his coat-of-arms made to the Earl of Suffolk (acting as Deputy Marshal to his cousin, the Duke of Norfolk, hereditary Earl Marshal but still a minor), Vanbrugh had provided a brief account of his family. It showed:

> That Giles Vanbrug quitting his native country for the enjoyment of the re-formed religion, retired to England, and having been bred a merchant, settled as such in London, in the parish of St Stephen, Walbrook, where he continued

until his death in 1646; and having purchased a vault in the church was buried in it. This Giles bore his ancestorial arms and crest, but had made no entry of them in the College of Arms.[2]

The matter of enquiry within the College was referred to Garter and to Clarenceux, and as Vanbrugh held the latter post a very quick confirmation was forthcoming. The herald and new knight had certainly 'ancestorial arms' of three barrulets on a fess with a demy lion in chief, 'quartered with the shield of his mother', daughter of a noble household. The first Giles and his wife Maria (Jacobs) had as their third son Giles (1631–1689), John Vanbrugh's father. After spending the years 1655–8 travelling in France and Italy, including a visit to Rome (the account of which must later have been most interesting to his son), Giles returned to England and in 1659 married Elizabeth Carleton, as her second husband. This introduction was possibly arranged by his brother William, who had married Dorothy Carleton, Elizabeth's sister, in 1652. It was only William who had known his father-in-law, Sir Dudley Carleton, for he died in 1654. He was the nephew of that illustrious diplomat, also Sir Dudley, who had travelled to embassies in Venice and The Hague in the reign of James I. He was a friend and patron of Rubens and enjoyed the favour in his later years of Charles I, whose Secretary of State he became in 1628. The King created him Viscount Dorchester in the same year.[3]

THE BOY

John Vanbrugh was born to Giles and Elizabeth in London, within the parish of St Nicholas Acons, in January 1664. He was baptized there on 24 January, presumably the day of his birth. His father had set up as a cloth merchant, but turned to sugar-baking (refining) after they left London in 1667 to live at Chester. This move was presumably on account of privations in London after the Plague and Great Fire, 1665–6. The boyhood of many past figures is often scantily recorded, and we know nothing of substance about John Vanbrugh before the mid-1680s. What this does is to feed speculation about him – what his abilities and interests were, where he may have been educated, or made journeys to, what he read, and what was sought out for study or pleasure. Did he attend the King's School, in Chester, or that founded by the 3rd Earl of Huntingdon at Ashby-de-la-Zouch, or even study with a private tutor? There is more conjecture than evidence, and more plausible assumption than established fact.[4]

It seems only sensible to assume that Giles Vanbrugh had a good command of the French language, befitting his Flemish Protestant origins, and that his son John became fluent, to a standard capable at a later date of translating French plays. Through his mother's family John Vanbrugh could also claim a relationship, however distant, to other noble families,[5] among them the Hastings, Earls of Huntingdon, and the Berties, Lords of Willoughby and Earls of Lindsey, and later, Dukes of Ancaster. The 1st Duke acted as godfather at the birth, in 1722, of the architect's son, also John (**2**).

In 1685 John Vanbrugh came of age, and started to think more carefully about his future. He wanted to journey further than the medieval city of Chester, although its walled silhouette may have always stayed in his mind, and to avoid having 'to bake sugar for the rest of his days'.[6] His mother at least probably approved of his ambition, a blend of action and spirit which came as much from her Carleton line as that of the Van Bruggs: or so she fondly thought.

THE SOLDIER

Theophilus Hastings, 7th Earl of Huntingdon (1650-1701), a volunteer in the French army in 1672, was the recipient of the earliest Vanbrugh letter traced to date, 28 December 1685.[7] The young man, referring to the Earl as his 'kinsman', thanked him for previous help and asked for employment. The Earl, ever intent on military matters, offered him a commission in his foot regiment, which was gazetted in his favour on 30 January 1686.[8] Vanbrugh had been disappointed at not being offered a post under the Earl's informal inspectorship of royal gardens.[9] They had not been effectively organized since the death of Hugh May in 1684, and this led, eventually, to a new post of 'Superintendent of all the King's gardens' in June 1689 to which the Earl of Portland was appointed.[10] As it was, the regiment was ordered out to help garrison Guernsey, and as that was a place where Vanbrugh did not wish to languish, possibly for many years, he resigned his commission in August 1686.

It was another group of kinsmen who took up the young man. One of his Bertie relatives, James, Earl of Abingdon was appointed High Steward of Oxford in January 1687. His bailiffs, of whom one was 'John Vanbrooke', were also given the freedom of the city. Times were troubled in James II's short reign, and the King removed the Earl and his bailiffs from office in February 1688. Moreover the intelligence reports were showing that William of Orange was preparing his Dutch forces to invade England. Vanbrugh had already left for France, and at some point, seemingly in late September 1688, he was arrested there.[11]

There has been considerable speculation about what Vanbrugh was doing abroad. He may well have gone sightseeing in the company of the likewise dismissed bailiffs, Robert Bertie, Lord Willoughby, and Peregrine Bertie, who had planned to meet in Paris in March 1688.[12] He alleged his arrest was for talking about William of Orange, and having no passport in time of war. He was then held as a hostage in exchange for one or other French spies in English custody. There seems some reason to assume

Vanbrugh was also spying. What seems as likely is that he was the pawn in a diplomatic 'game'; but he was in any case a 'poor hostage, having few claims to notoriety, or possession of sensitive information'. There is nevertheless an uneasy fact to consider, as Sir John Summerson has noted: the privilege given to Vanbrugh to build his house in 1699 in the ruins of Whitehall Palace. He was allowed to use unlimited quantities of rubble, which may have been a reward for services to the Crown. What were they? – secret missions to France?[13] Certainly the Vanbrugh household for some years past had needed to listen to the details of Giles Vanbrugh's wild and complicated scheme to assault the Eternal City of Rome – where he had spent a year earlier in his life – and take back all the ancient manuscripts gathered at the Vatican Library. Giles's letter of 28 December 1678 about this to the Bishop of London[14] made much of surprise, secrecy and 'Rebellions fomented ... by the Jesuiticall Romanists'. Giles Vanbrugh died in 1689, whilst his son John was in a French prison: his will devised to the absent John two of the 14 allocations of its provisions.

The diplomatic tussle between William III's officers and those of Louis XIV became active in 1691. Vanbrugh was to be exchanged for a French officer, but Louis XIV put difficulties in the way – wanting back, perhaps, Martin Bertillier who was in Newgate Prison on suspicion of being a spy. Vanbrugh's movements about Calais on foot were restricted, and he was transferred to the château of Vincennes. He was soon offering bail, to be allowed the liberty of its courtyard.[15] All there was for him to do each day was to petition the French King, and perhaps as a result of these efforts he was transferred in January 1692 to the Bastille. It was then, in February 1692, that Narcissus Luttrell, the Cambridge annalist and bibliographer, recorded in his *A Brief Historicall Relation of State Affairs from September 1678 to April 1714* (printed 1857): 'Mr Vanbrook, Mr Goddard, and Mr North ... clapt up in the Bastille, suspected to be spies'.

There was at least a tactical pretext for France to so regard them, 'tho' hitherto there is no ground for suspicion', Lord Nottingham, Secretary of State, wrote in September 1692 to his colleague, William Blathwayt. Thomas, Earl of Aylesbury in his own memoirs noted that the prisoners included 'Mr Vanbrook, the famous poet since, who composed in the Bastille his most ingenious play "The Provok'd Wife"'. It was imprisonment of a sort, and before and after it may have allowed, however fleetingly, some visual acquaintance with French architecture, especially that in Paris. Vanbrugh nevertheless wrote to Blathwayt himself on 26 August 1692,[16] asking perhaps desperately that the King would hasten their release from France 'that our Liberty may be employ'd in his service'. It had not cheered him at all to hear that his brother Dudley had unfortunately killed the colonel of his regiment in a duel. There was a need to be free, to head the family. Finally, after a few more months of interchange and counterplay, Vanbrugh was released on bail, but another four months drifted on before they could sail for England. He, and Goddard, a nephew of Sir Samuel Dashwood, arrived in England on 1 April 1693 either at Dover or Folkestone, and were at once arrested. Lord Nottingham wrote hastily to the mayors of both towns explaining their four years of enforced stay in France, and ordering their good treatment and release.

Vanbrugh was back, and free, but with no real job of work it was hardly an enviable state. There was the sinecure post of Auditor for the Southern Division of the Duchy of Lancaster, a post seemingly given him while he was away in prison. The Chancellor of the Duchy was his friend Robert Bertie, Lord Willoughby, created 1st Duke of Ancaster in 1715. Vanbrugh had been with him in Holland before his own arrest. The Duchy post had been kept warm by Tobias Legros, as deputy of 'John Vanbrough', but when Vanbrugh was back Lord Willoughby eased him forward into receiving the dues of the post. He held it until more important matters came his way in 1702, but as late as 1715 he was paid £5 as an arrear of taxes, due to him as Auditor in 1694.

The Auditor must have been made of stern stuff, for in 1695 he again involved himself in military activities. He spent a short time at sea – in the service of Peregrine Osborne, Marquis of Carmarthen, the son of the 1st Duke of Leeds, who succeeded in 1712. Vanbrugh saw action in the unsuccessful attack on the French naval port of Brest[17], less covert in style than his service hitherto. After this he became a lieutenant in another regiment – for eight days – and then became a captain of marines at £180 a year, under Lord Berkeley. His Lordship, who had been a member of the provisional government after the flight of James II, accepted Vanbrugh on the recommendation of Lord Carmarthen. It was the last day of 1695.

THE DRAMATIST

There was perhaps no sudden point or particular day when Vanbrugh decided he was a dramatist[18] rather than a soldier, or when he put architecture before drama. They stayed as strong, intermingled parts of his life: an abiding interest in the embattled house, mighty outworks, and enormous gateways with obelisks were as relevant as turning his pen to translation, or invention. He had written disconnected fragments in the Bastille which were later worked up as his third play. Colley Cibber, son of the Huguenot sculptor Caius Gabriel Cibber, a young actor and dramatist, recorded that when Vanbrugh had been 'but an ensign' he made a seemingly fortunate encounter with one of the joint Patentees of the Theatre Royal in Drury Lane.[19] Through faulty management its leading players had gone off to set up in Lincoln's Inn Fields, and to open with a new play *Love for Love* by the leading dramatist, William Congreve.

The young, unknown Drury Lane actors, Cibber among them, were left to fend alone. Cibber was intent on seeing his own comedy *Love's Last Shift* put into production. It became a hard-rehearsed immediate success, a fact which did not elude the watchful Vanbrugh, aspiring dramatist, with much writing and thought in the Bastille to launch him also in a new direction. Writing hard, he handed in *The Relapse, or Virtue in Danger*. Cibber's 'Sir Novelty Fashion' was retained but changed into Lord Foppington. The first words, spoken by Miss Cross, noted the haste of its creation:

> Ladys, this Play in too much haste was writ
> To be o'ercharg'd with either Plot or Wit;
> 'Twas Got, Conceiv'd, and Born in six Weeks space....

But the audiences applauded loudly at the ravishing of Amanda by the drunken Worthy, and greatly enjoyed watching the affected Lord Foppington. This first effort had succeeded well beyond being a mere sequel to Cibber, but its fickle dealing with morality soon roused the critics to action. They were addressed by Vanbrugh in the preface to the printed version issued after the performance, as:

> the Saints (your thorough-pac'd ones I mean, with screw'd Faces and Wry Mouths) ... They love nothing but their Altars and Themselves ... and are as quarrelsome in their Religion, as other People are in their Drink ...

His next play, by chance more chaste, called *Aesop*, was put on by Christopher Rich within a few weeks of *The Relapse*. It had:

> No Hero, no Romance, no Plot, no Show,
> No Rape, no Bawdy, no Intrigue, no Beau –.

and consequently, no devotees. It was however Vanbrugh's first translation from the French. Vanbrugh may have seen Boursault's original, *Ésope à la Ville*, in Paris.

Vanbrugh was already tilting again at his pious critics, with a song in his sketch, based on his writings of the Bastille years: when worked up, Lord Halifax asked him to put it on at the actor-manager Thomas Betterton's theatre in Lincoln's Inn Fields, with the good company that had left Skipwith and Rich at Drury Lane. He titled it *The Provok'd Wife*:

> When my Head's full of wine,
> I o'erflow with Design,
> And know no Penal Laws that can curb me:
> Whate'er I devise,
> Seems good in my Eyes,
> And Religion ne'er dares to disturb me.

It was a fine song for an intending architect: and a fine song for his convivial Kit-Cat friends who met as a club to talk, argue, and eat Christo-

pher Cat's fine, designed mutton pies. The play was Vanbrugh's master-
piece and yet he knew nothing of the role of a harsh lewd husband (Sir
John Brute) bored by his wife who in turn would cuckold him. It says
much for the level of his earthy powers of invention, that riding over the
charges levelled at *The Relapse*, he could produce work that earned Pope's
double-edged aesthetic judgement: 'How Van wants grace, who never
wanted wit.' The critics were to be again tilted at, obliquely, through the
words of Constant, in *The Provok'd Wife*:

> Virtue consists in Goodness, Honour,
> Gratitude, Sincerity and Pity, and not in peevish, snarling,
> strait-laced Chastity.

But his writing had intensified criticism, which came to a head in 1698
with Jeremy Collier's *A Short View of the Immorality and Profaneness of the
English Stage*.

Collier was a Puritan non-juring clergyman; he had come to note in
1696 when he mounted the scaffold at Tyburn to bless two Jacobites who
had plotted to kill King William III. He was outlawed – at least tech-
nically – for his action, but came out of hiding 'when the pleasures of
martyrdom began to wane'.[20] His *Short View* attacked all dramatists, but
particularly Vanbrugh, indicting him for being bawdy, blasphemous, and
incompetent. He devoted a chapter to *The Relapse*, but became absurd in
his charges about the bawdiness therein, the blasphemy (when the plays
were only light stuff) and incompetence, when he could show no supre-
macy in his own pages. Like all scandal Collier's diatribe was an uninten-
tional best-seller. Dryden ignored it, magnanimously, but Wycherley,
Congreve and Vanbrugh all took up their pens to reply, with Vanbrugh's
riposte at least having the longest title: *A Short Vindication of the Relapse and
The Provok'd Wife from Immorality and Profaneness*. It had been held, in the
Puritan view of biblical texts, that vice was but one step away from evil,
and Collier's timely attack thus prevailed: the magistrates took their cue,
and prosecuted three leading actors, Betterton among them, 'for using
indecent expressions in some late plays, particularly *The Provok'd Wife*'.
Vanbrugh did not write another play for three years.

When Vanbrugh turned his mind again to the theatre it had to compete
with the claims of patrons more anxious to see buildings rise than curtains.
In five further plays he only worked up clever versions of the earlier work
of others – Fletcher's *The Pilgrim* of 1621, performed in 1700, with some
parts added by the aged Dryden, *The False Friend* (1702) in which Collier's
attack was flouted by the inclusion of an attempted rape, the words having
been translated by Le Sage from a Spanish play, and by Vanbrugh from
Le Sage's French edition. His *The Country House* (1698) which, alas, says
nothing about those he built, was taken from Dancourt's *La Maison de*

Campagne (1688, performed 1698). Whilst Vanbrugh was still a military man, Lord Carlisle was about to ask him to design Castle Howard. By contrast the play presented Mr Barnard, self-made, who had been silly enough to buy a house – Dancourt was adept at setting out the stumbles in his efforts at aggrandisement. The Earl of Carlisle used Vanbrugh well; through long lineage he was grand, and through great political experience had not stumbled – yet.

In 1704 Vanbrugh collaborated with William Congreve and William Walsh in translating a play by Molière, and retitling it *Squire Trelooby*. It was done with great speed, each writing an act, and finished in two days. Congreve disowned it eventually as he regarded it as an attack on some people of importance. Cibber admired the 'spirit, ease, and readiness' which Vanbrugh could summon to produce plays fast. The rival theatre companies were however struggling, arguing with each other, and with managers who were slow to pay them, and never the full amounts due.

It had been borne in upon Vanbrugh on many occasions as he tried to stage his plays, tussling with managers and actors and worrying about small stages, that his own theatre would be desirable. How did 'The Queen's Theatre, or Italian Opera House' in the Haymarket, come into being? Even those who gathered for *The Loves of Ergasto* on the opening night, Easter Monday, 9 April 1705, must have wondered at the size and gilded splendour of all around them.

In 1703 Vanbrugh had joined with Betterton and Congreve to suggest that they should build a new theatre in Haymarket. Vanbrugh would design it: all three would manage it. Many of their friends in the Kit-Cat Club promised to subscribe 100 guineas each in return for free entrance for life, but apart from giving confidence few did so. Nevertheless Queen Anne ordered a 'New Company ... under stricter Govermt and Regulations ...' with 'especiall trust and confidence in ... John Vanbrugh and Willm Congreve Esqrs ...'.[21] At once the Society for Reformation of Manners, adherents of Collier's strictures, wrote to Archbishop Tenison about the theatre being in charge of 'Mr *Vanbrook*, the known Character of which Gentleman has very much alarm'd us'. The prelate avoided the battle, and Lady Anne Sunderland laid the foundation stone on 18 April 1704 of 'The Queen's Theatre, or Italian Opera House', a venture in which Vanbrugh had put all his fervent hopes, and a deal of money. Meanwhile, at a more distant site, Lady Sunderland's father, the Duke of Marlborough, was soon to be engaged in a struggle, but one which was to affect Vanbrugh's career as significantly – that of the battle of Blenheim in August 1704.

Inside his theatre, Vanbrugh's striving after grand architecture[22] overlooked a normal requirement – for good acoustics. The theatre was soon known to be deficient in this vital respect, but Vanbrugh still had to meet the same expenses even if the audiences were declining. In an attempt to continue the repertoire, in the summer of 1705 he produced another of his translations from Dancourt, and titled it *The Confederacy*. It had all the sparkling quality of *The Provok'd Wife*, but the audience had to strain again to hear it. Voices were lost up in the great proscenium arch; the play folded after a week, and the dispirited company needed a different dialogue, urgently, and with someone who could hear it. In 1708, after writing one more play (awkwardly titled in the circumstances) *The Mistake*, Vanbrugh concluded negotiations and sold out to the impresario Owen Swiney (or McSwiny). Disappointed, he wrote to the Earl of Manchester on 11 May 1708:

> I have parted with my whole concern to Mr Swiney; only reserving my Rent: So that he is entire possessor of the Opera, And most People think, will manage it better than any body....[23]

The rest of the letter was concerned with Swiney's employment of two women opera singers, Nicolini and Santini, whom Lord Manchester was ready to persuade to come to London. Improvements in structure were also made to remedy the acoustics. Vanbrugh further apprised the Earl, on 27 July 1708[24], that he had 'lost so Much Money by the opera this Last Winter, that I was glad to get quit of it ...'. Some of the trouble, he owned, had been because he was too busy, and had to leave matters to managers. Nevertheless Vanbrugh kept an interest in the management and leases for at least ten more years, to the time of his marriage, in 1719. It had been, until then, his only 'affair'.

Vanbrugh took the line in his plays that they could not 'have offended any honest Gentleman of the Town, whose Friendship of good Word is worth the having.' He loved to expound in them the doubtful vagaries of low life and marital disagreement – yet did so charged with his own good humour. In Nicholas Rowe's poem[25] about a reconciliation between Jacob Tonson and Congreve, the former is made to say that Vanbrugh was 'a most SWEET-NATURED gentleman, and pleasant'. He was not, moreover, endlessly probing 'the deep emotions of mankind, having in him 'an ingrained contempt for all cant and humbug' and 'a considerable amount of the spirit of comedy'.[26] He would have liked to have known that, after his death, Cibber completed his unfinished play *A Journey to London*, and produced it, in 1728, as *The Provok'd Husband*. He might well have been amused also at the probing of his writings in many recent dissertations[27], or to know that the adventures of Sir John Brute, first a clergyman, then (after Collier's attack) dressed as a lady, Lord Foppington, Clarissa Gripe and her maid Flippanta, and the array of other delightful characters still attract us when one of his plays is performed.

THE ARCHITECT

In *The Provok'd Wife* Vanbrugh had first cast Sir John Brute as a drunken clergyman. This offended Collier, and it irritated a much more profound churchman, the later Dean of St Patrick's, Dublin, Jonathan Swift. A brilliant satirist, Swift penned some verses[28] in return in 1703 (published later): on 'Vanbrug's House', which made its owner regret he had ever crossed the cloth. Not only was he castigated for taking a French play, and stealing from it the plot and every joke, but also that his house was so small, a 'Goose-Pye' that could be trailed around like that of a snail 'or harnessed to a nag, at ease'.

> ... Now Poets from all quarters ran
> To see the house of brother Van:
> Look'd high and low, walk'd often round,
> But no such house was to be found:
> One asks the watermen hard by,
> 'Where may the Poet's palace lie?'
> Another of the Thames inquires
> If he has seen its gilded spires?
> At length they in the rubbish spy
> A thing resembling a Goose-Pye.

It was masterly invective, and was followed up in 1706 with 'The History of Vanbrug's House', which noted, correctly, but amid many biting lines:

> Van's genius, without thought or lecture,
> Is hugely turn'd to architecture.

In 1710 Swift wrote to Stella that he had dined at Sir Richard Temple's with both Congreve and Vanbrugh:

> Vanburgh, I believe I told you, had a long quarrel with me about those verses on his house, but we were very civil and cold. Lady Marlborough used to tease him with them, which made him angry, though he be a good-natured fellow.

Swift eventually was sorry for his unkindness. In the intervening years his 'Man of Wit, and of Honour' proved that he was an architect well capable of rearing much more than a snail's slimy house, or a 'Goose-Pye' in the ashes of Whitehall. Both he and Pope were handsome in their regrets at 'Railery' in the joint preface to Swift's *Miscellanies in Prose*, 1727, quoted at my chapter-head.

It used to be thought that at the age of 19 (in 1683) Vanbrugh had paid a visit to France. There is no evidence for this, and while he was certainly there in 1688 it is only possible to speculate what, under the eventual conditions of imprisonment, he saw of French architecture – or indeed how he used it if he saw anything. All studies of Vanbrugh – this included – provide photographs of Versailles, the court of the Invalides, the Palais Luxembourg, and so on, to draw attention to borrowed motifs. As important however was Vanbrugh's long-held interest in medieval architecture, the theories of Alberti, and the villas of Palladio. We know he had Martin's 1650 edition of Palladio, and Wren and Hawksmoor had excellent libraries to supplement what he possessed. To that was added a rich imagination and a bold originality. He was, 'as an architect, a brilliant novice' who needed to co-operate with the well-versed Nicholas Hawksmoor, who had been assisting that 'miracle of a youth' the Surveyor-General Christopher Wren from the late 1670s. The nature of the relationship with Hawksmoor has been well summarized by Sir John Summerson[29], who notes Vanbrugh's outstanding contributions to English architecture: in the early work at Castle Howard, playing 'that game of lively but carefully reticulated relationships, in height and in recession', and in the last houses, without Hawksmoor's help, pursuing 'the idea of pure mass-relationship as the grand means of effect, with classical elements thrust into the composition at points where they could strike the most telling and even bizarre notes.'

It was due almost entirely to the Earl of Carlisle, at the centre of power as Lord Treasurer, that Vanbrugh was appointed to the Comptrollership of the Board of Works. The Earl had been much irritated by his erstwhile architect at Castle Howard, William Talman, who had been Comptroller since 1689. Talman had also been distinctly awkward to Wren when new buildings at Hampton Court had fallen down in December 1689. Carlisle did not therefore renew Talman's patent at the accession of Queen Anne, and on 20 May 1702, at a meeting attended by the Queen, Vanbrugh was appointed in his place.[30] A year later Carlisle, then acting as Deputy Marshal in the minority of the Duke of Norfolk, and against much opposition in the College of Arms had Vanbrugh 'touched' as a Herald[31], and he was also appointed one of the Board of Directors of Greenwich Hospital in the same year. It was as auspicious a start to his official career as designing Castle Howard (see Chapter II) had been to that of his acceptance as an architect.

He was still a year or two away from the time when Swift's barbs would sting, and remind all of the Earl's indulgence to him:

> Van, (for 'tis fit the Reader know it)
> Is both a Herald and a Poet;
> No wonder then, if nicely skill'd
> In each capacity to Build:
> As Herald, he can in a Day
> Repair a House gone to decay;
> Or by Atchievements, Arms, Device
> Erect a new one in a Trice; ...

In 1704-5 involvement with a powerful patron was secured when Vanbrugh was chosen to build Blenheim, the lavish palace at Woodstock to be given as a mark of royal favour to the Duke of Marlborough for his victories over the armies of Louis XIV. The complicated progress of its erection is told in Chapter II: it is sufficient here to note that the commission made Vanbrugh the leading architect of his age. He also took much of the main workload within the Board of Works, and this encouraged him to think he would soon be chosen to succeed the ageing Wren as its Surveyor-General. He was stopped short in that process by Wren himself, who had been chosen by the Duchess of Marlborough in a direct snub to Vanbrugh, to build Marlborough House. Wren used his son Christopher to assist him there in the belief it would position the young man to succeed him as Surveyor-General. In the final event Wren didn't lay down his office of his own will; he was dismissed, shabbily, following the political appointment of William Benson in 1718. Vanbrugh later owned, in two letters, one of 18 March 1713 to the Duke of Marlborough[32], and another of 29 November 1719[33] to Jacob Tonson, at Paris, that he was disappointed at not being made Surveyor then, and that he could have had the post before: 'but refus'd it, out of Tenderness to Sr. Chr: Wren . . .'.

In 1710 the Tories under Robert Harley, Earl of Oxford, returned to political power in a country weary of war, but roused by the impeachment and conviction of Dr Henry Sacheverell. He had attacked the government and the Hanoverian succession in a sermon preached at St Paul's Cathedral in November 1709. Something of the humdrum catholicity of Board of Works tasks Wren and Vanbrugh had to arrange can be gauged from that of the setting-up of scaffolding for Sacheverell's trial in Westminster Hall, including a place at which the Queen and her ladies could attend incognito. The Duke of Marlborough and his Duchess, dismissed by the Queen, had gone into the country (later abroad in voluntary exile) and work was soon to be halted at Blenheim. It was already at a difficult stage and at this point Vanbrugh must have looked with interest on a new Tory proposal, graciously approved by the Queen – set out in an Act of Parliament of 1711 – for building 50 new churches in London.

The papers relating to the new churches have been published.[34] In brief, by their building the new administration intended to show they had faith in the Established Church. The money was to come from new duty on sea-coal coming into London, a measure which had already been used in the building of St Paul's Cathedral. The terms of the Act were to be administered by Commissioners appointed from the government and church; Wren, his son, Vanbrugh, and the Groom Porter and gentleman-architect, Thomas Archer were also elected. Nicholas Hawksmoor and William Dickinson, Wren's assistant on the rebuilding of the City churches, were appointed at the second meeting to be Surveyors to the Commissioners. They were charged with finding sites, surveying them, and soon it seemed all competent architects were busy preparing plans, and having wooden models made. Dickinson did little in his post, and was succeeded in 1713 by James Gibbs.

Vanbrugh put forward eight 'Proposals' on how the churches were to be built, 'in a plain, but Just and Noble Stile', without many divisions and breaks, or the gaiety of ornaments 'as may be proper in a Luxurious Palace'. They were to be free-standing and placed carefully, be 'Accommodated and Adorned with Portico's' and be solid in 'Wall and Manner of their Construction'. The seeming relationship of these and other proposals by Vanbrugh to Alberti's theories and to the fourth book of Palladio's *Quattro Libri*, discussing Temples, has already been discussed.[35] Vanbrugh had considered such matters for his 'Proposals', and for the designs of two churches he submitted: one for St Mary-le-Strand (a design by James Gibbs was preferred)[36], and one for St George, Bloomsbury. This was accepted, but superseded some months later by Hawksmoor's design. As a slightly older and much more experienced man, Hawksmoor had often acted to Vanbrugh as 'an organizer, a draughtsman and a designer'. With Vanbrugh's acquiescence his designs for six churches were accepted in stages by the Commission. They were a worthy continuation of a distinguished career which had already contributed much of the detail of Castle Howard and Blenheim.

The manuscript of the 'Proposals'[37] had included as its 18th that churches should be free, in or near them, 'from the Inhumane custome of being made Burial Places for the Dead ...' and that instead cemeteries should be provided at a distance, 'Handsomely and regularly wall'd in, and planted with Trees ... to make a Solemn Distinction between one Part and another.' The dead could then be 'more honourably remember'd by Lofty and Noble Mausoleums, erected over them in Freestone ...'. Vanbrugh cited this practice at the English cemetery at 'Suratt', the Indian trading centre of the East India Company, which had 'been an English colony for more than a hundred years when he ... made a sketch of its cemetery, apparently derived from some view he had seen.'[38]

Sir John Vanbrugh, from 'Proposals for the Fifty Churches' 1711; sketch of an ideal cemetery.

A supplementary Act of 1712, following that of 1711, which had set up the Commission, did in fact stop the practice of church burials.

The starting and stopping of building work at Blenheim had a serious effect on the workforce living nearby in Woodstock. As they danced the night away at the laying of the Blenheim foundation stone on 18 June 1705, they could not have suspected that, eventually, they would be laid off for long periods, or would be penurious creditors sinking beneath the vast Blenheim debt. This situation had affected the Marlborough in-terest in Woodstock in the 1710 election, and as it was necessary to avoid the town going Tory at the next one the Duke decided he would pay to pave the streets for the convenience of its inhabitants. Vanburgh wrote to the mayor on 25 January 1713[39] advising him of this, and it was also in his own mind to design alterations to make the Town Hall larger. Unfor-tunately, by an ill-written name the letter to the 'Mayor' was carried to one 'Major', who was acquainted with Lord Oxford. The letter had con-tained the scurrilous indication that the paving would have been carried out by the Duke long since 'but for the continual *plague and bitter persecution he has most barbarously followed with for two years past'*. When knowledge of Vanbrugh's misdirected letter reached Lord Oxford the reaction was pre-dictable. On 31 March 1713, Vanbrugh was dismissed from his Comp-trollership at the Board of Works, and the Queen vetoed his election at the College of Arms from Clarenceux to the more prestigious and lucrative post of Garter. In fact, as Vanbrugh wrote on 16 January 1715 to the Duke of Marlborough[40] the Queen had thought his behaviour 'had been such in writing that Letter to Woodstock, that now she had done with me – That was her expression.'

The Comptrollership of the Works was now vacant and other contes-tants petitioned for attention: William Talman, Thomas Archer, Nicholas Hawksmoor, and the younger Christopher Wren. But times of upheaval also allow time to ponder reorganization; Harley made no appointment, and the death of the Queen on 1 August 1714 rendered all posts at the pleasure of George I. At the outset of this chapter we referred to Van-brugh's knighthood, and his re-appointment in January 1715 as Comp-troller. In June an interesting revival of the old post of Sur-intendent of Buildings and Gardens was made by his appointment at a salary of £400 a year as 'Surveyor of Gardens and Waters'.[41] It was all part of the changes which came to the Board of Works by the Orders of April 1715, with considerable tightening of procedure, and new appointments as others lapsed. The suggested revisions had been pointed out in a list of 'Heads for a new Settlement of the Office of Works' which Vanbrugh had been asked to prepare the previous November by Lord Halifax, the new First Lord of the Treasury.

'Lord Halifax's Orders', as they were known, acted as the Board's rule book for just over three years. Vanbrugh's regular attendance at its meetings[42] act as a useful supplement to what is known of the dates of his visits to his private commissions. He saw himself not only as the author of the 1715 revisions but as the one who carried them into effect under Wren's nominal chairmanship. He wrote as much to the Earl of Sunderland and the Duke of Newcastle in July 1718 and May 1719 respectively, indicating that he had 'lessen'd the Expence, ten thousand pounds a year'.[43] The actual figures made, perhaps, more sombre reading than this special pleading by the Comptroller allowed.[44] He had positioned himself well to be the next Surveyor-General following Wren's expected retirement, but underestimated the political jobbery to which he had long been subjected.

In April 1718 Wren's dismissal as Surveyor-General was announced, and William Benson, an architectural patron, with an interest in hydraulics – this had endeared him to the future George I, when he had designed the waterworks at Herrenhausen – was appointed as Surveyor-General. He was quickly persuading anyone in power who would listen that there were grave deficiencies in the Board's administration. No effort was spared to unseat Vanbrugh, who wrote to the Duke of Newcastle about the charges which, he thought, made him appear, in the King's eyes, 'a very bad Officer'. The letter[45] is undated but must have been sent near the time when the Board was dissolved, on 21 August 1718. Within the week Hawksmoor, and other Vanbrugh adherents, like Henry Joynes and Thomas Kynaston, were dismissed.

Colen Campbell, the rising 'propagandist of the Palladian movement', as author of *Vitruvius Britannicus* (two of three projected volumes had already appeared, 1715 and 1717) was appointed the Surveyor's Deputy on 2 September 1718.[46] Vanbrugh retaliated by stating that Kynaston would act as his deputy, and ignored the implied insult when Benson appointed the Duchess of Marlborough's 'Oracle', the furniture maker, James Moore (*c.* 1672–1726) as the Purveyor. Moore had completed Blenheim after the Duchess's final quarrel with her architect. Both had thought quarrels were a pastime without end, but those raging in the Board of Works were to cause problems for the protagonists.

The Master Mason, Benjamin Jackson, a Talman protégé, who had evaded the Board's regulations on numerous occasions, and was no friend of Vanbrugh's, came, almost unwittingly, to his relief. Benson and Campbell had in a report condemned certain buildings in and adjacent to the House of Lords to be in danger of collapse. Jackson was ordered to 'view the walls' with others, and report to the House on oath. He did so, to the effect that they were sound, and then used the opportunity to score hard: he had only recently condemned Benson's dishonest contractual practices (from which he had been excluded). Vanbrugh joined in the attack, and Sir Jacob Bancks, whom Benson had denounced in a pamphlet for advocating 'the Divine uncontrolled power of Princes', hurried in with a scurrilous pamphlet attack. Adding up Benson's previous attempts to assert rights over Crown possessions – the Isle of Portland stone quarries – the Lords ordered his removal, and drew the King's attention to his behaviour. Struggling hard, with legal disputes and bargaining all around him, Benson was dismissed on 16 April 1719, but did not surrender formally until July 17.[47] He had brought the Board of Works to a point of despair, out of favour with the House of Lords, and may have done so from a 'violent Disorder of Mind', which it was later alleged (1741) he had suffered.

Further despair came to the normally ebullient Vanbrugh when, mindful of having been passed over once for the post of Surveyor-General, the now vacant post was given to yet another with inadequate experience, Thomas Hewett, a staunch Whig, and an amateur architect.[48] Vanbrugh wrote to the Duke of Newcastle on 6 August 1719[49] that it was difficult to 'help this Pill downe, which is a little Bitter, now I come just to the time (and disgrace) of Swallowing it ... 'tis one of the hardest pieces of Fortune, that ever fell to anybody ...'. Even his efforts to have Hawksmoor reinstated came to no avail, as nominees of Sir Thomas Hewett (he had been knighted in November 1719) were preferred. The tenure was undistinguished. Hewitt died in the same year as Vanbrugh (1726) having blocked him from those final rewarding years in the highest architectural office the King could bestow. Vanbrugh had never agreed readily to taking second place: it had always irked him that the post of Garter King of Arms had eluded him, but perhaps in view of his inexperience in heraldry there was good cause. He had consoled himself by having houses to build, and with other more personal matters. One of these had been his marriage.

THE HUSBAND AND FATHER

Henrietta Maria Yarburgh, Vanburgh's intended wife, had been born in 1693 at Snaith, Yorkshire and was baptized at St Lawrence, York, the church she chose later for her wedding. There is an oral family tradition that as a young girl Henrietta Maria had served in the household of Queen Anne. This seems to be a confusion with her aunt, also named Henrietta Maria, but the Yarburgh family had given devoted service to several monarchs.[50] Henrietta's grandfather, Sir Thomas Yarburgh, was, as a young man, a groom of the bedchamber to both King Charles I and Charles II, as well as being a Commissioner for the Hearth Tax. His eldest son and heir James, Henrietta's father, was a godson of James II, and a page of honour to the King. James's younger brother, Blague, was a page of honour to Charles II, and three of his sisters served as maids of honour: Henrietta Maria (mentioned above as aunt to Vanbrugh's future wife) served in the household of Queen Catherine both as Queen and as Dowager, and in that of Queen Mary – she was given £2,000 by the King in 1686 as her marriage portion to Sir Marmaduke Wyvill; Rosamonda was a maid of honour to Queen Anne in 1702–4; and the youngest sister, Alice, was introduced to court by her maternal aunt, Henrietta, 2nd Countess of Godolphin, and likewise became a maid of honour to Queen Anne.

The family connections[51], and those with the 1st Earl and Countess of Godolphin (Lord Godolphin was Queen Anne's Treasurer and had married, like Sir Thomas Yarburgh, a Blagge daughter) ensured the continuity of this long service. James Yarburgh, as well as loyal service to his godfather, James II, became a Colonel in the Guards, and also acted as aide-de-camp to the Duke of Marlborough. He married Anne Hesketh; and had seven sons and three daughters, of whom Henrietta Maria was the eldest. She was a great-niece of the Countess of Godolphin, and a second cousin to Lady Harriet Churchill. Vanbrugh had been asked by one of Harriet's grandmothers, Sarah, Duchess of Marlborough to 'match' her in marriage (p. 47) to his friend, Thomas Duke of Newcastle. They did marry in 1717, and the happiness of the union may have led Vanburgh to also consider marrying some two years later.

Vanbrugh may have first met Henrietta Maria on some court occasion or met her in York when he was staying at Castle Howard. Her mother Anne was co-heiress to her own brother, and when Snaith Hall burned down about 1707, the family moved to Heslington Hall, a mile or two from the centre of York. James lived on there until his death in 1728. His wife, Henrietta Maria's mother, predeceased him in April 1718, a few months before his daughter's marriage to Sir John Vanbrugh. 'Dear Van' had 'loved' a Yarburgh once before, in 1713, according to Lady Mary Wortley Montagu, an inveterate gossip, but it has been suggested that this was Faith Yarburgh, his wife's only maiden aunt.[52] Vanbrugh referred firmly to Henrietta Maria as his 'Heslington lady' in a letter of 1717 to the Duke of Newcastle. We know that Vanbrugh stayed on occasion in Yorkshire with the Robinson family, as well as spending time at Castle Howard. John Aislabie, Chancellor of the Exchequer, who was impeached at the time of the South Sea Bubble collapse, had a sister, Mary, who married Sir William Robinson of Newby (Baldersby), Yorkshire. She wrote to their son, Metcalfe '... we have had dined here Mr Vanbrook and all ye broaken officers in town', and later, 'yesterday at Lady Vanbrugh's I had nothing to do but criticise in my own mind Sr John's wonderfull taste in Architecture felicitating myself upon yr having none of his thick walls to pull down ...'.[53] At 'Lady Vanbrugh's' probably meant Greenwich Castle (**99–100**), and whilst the letters are undated they are presumably of *c.* 1720, in view of the mention of Lady Vanbrugh, and references to Metcalfe's building at Baldersby, started in that year under Colen Campbell's direction.[54]

The couple having decided to marry, Vanbrugh moved to Castle Howard in December 1718. It was snowy and at Christmas this bound him to Lord Carlisle's 'great fine house', and he was unable to meet the Duke of Newcastle at Nottingham Castle. He was in the mood to marry, as he wrote, 'to keep myself warm' (p. 59), and busied himself with a round of dinners, visits to the York Assembly, to neighbours like Lord Irwin, and then moved into York, to the George Inn, for the wedding. This took place on 14 January 1719 at St Lawrence, York, the church where Henrietta Maria, who was then 26, had, as noted, been baptized in 1693. Only the west tower of the church now stands: it contains an inscription to Henrietta Maria's mother, following her death in childbirth the previous April (1718). It has been assumed that as Vanbrugh described himself in the register as 'of Castle Howard' that Lord Carlisle was his best man.[55] He spared less than a week for his honeymoon, for the Duke of Newcastle still needed him to sort out the building works at Nottingham Castle. It must have pleased him that in his letter to the Duke of 24 January 1719,[56] he could refer to his wife 'being pretty near related to the Dutchess', and that he knew 'all will be well' with their marriage. But his old friend Jacob Tonson, he owned further, 'will be frightned out of his Witts and his Religion too, when he hears I'm gone at last ... I was the last Man left, between him and Ruin.'

On Vanbrugh's side at least – there is little evidence of Henrietta's views – the marriage did seem happy. He wrote to Tonson, at last, on 1 July 1719[57] about what he had done, indicating that his view of marriage had:

> confirmed (as far as Six months practice goes) my Old Opinion was right; That whatever there was of good or bad in Marriage; it was fitter to end our life with than begin it. . . .

On 11 August 1719[58] Vanbrugh wrote again to the Duke of Newcastle, and mentioned the premature birth of a daughter: 'a Bit of a Girle popping into the World, three months before its time. And so the business is all to do over again.' On 5 November 1719[59] he mentioned to Tonson that he had 'a good humour'd wife (and) a quiet house ...', and in the following year Lady Vanbrugh gave birth to their first son.

In the family Bible and Book of Common Prayer of 1629 (**2**), given her by John's mother, Elizabeth, Henrietta recorded the birth date, 20 October 1720[60], her son's name, Charles, and the names of his illustrious godparents, Henrietta the Countess of Godolphin and 2nd Duchess of Marlborough (in her own right), the 3rd Earl of Carlisle, and her brother, Colonel James Yarburgh.

Whilst Lady Vanbrugh had been heavy with her unborn child there were occasions when Vanbrugh dined out alone, with their friends. In September 1720, the month before Charles was born, he had been with Lord Carlisle and a group of companions to hear music in the Duke of Chandos's Chapel at Cannons, and on to dinner with the Duke. The day after he was off with the same group to the Duke's town house: Brigadier Watkins would have a 'Shoulder of Mutton' ready for them, and he told the Duke of Newcastle (on 15 September 1720),[61] 'We shan't fail to drink your Grace's and the Lady's health in (I daresay) the Best Wine in your cellar, As your very Obedient humble Servants, particularly J VAN-BRUGH.'

In financial matters Vanbrugh was still in debt over the Opera House. His demands for payment of arrears at Blenheim had met with little result: indeed he had to make a long 'Justification' of his actions in 1721 to the Court of Exchequer, and had sent his paper 'to all the Lords in Towne, as well as given it to the King, Prince & Princess'.[62] Whilst the case was lost by the Marlboroughs, Vanbrugh had also lost money in the South Sea affair, at a time when the Duchess of Marlborough, acting quickly, had got out and increased her fortune by £100,000. It was time to forget and go north to Yorkshire. With young Charles they set out in July 1721 and came finally to Heslington, with Vanbrugh himself going on to Castle Howard. There were still many things to do there, for it was, as he wrote to the Duke of Newcastle, on 8 August 1721,[63] 'the Top Seat and Garden of England'. This was the period when as well as visiting at Castle Howard he found time, as he told the Duke, to be in York for 'a Race every day, and a Ball every night', and to journey north, to Seaton Delaval and Lumley Castle.

Within six months, at the start of the New Year, there was further happiness at the birth of a second son, John, on 14 January 1722.[64] The Duchess of Newcastle, the Duke of Ancaster, and Lord Cobham stood faith as godparents at the font. Their pleasure in the kicking baby, and the extent of their future commitment was however to be limited, for John died in a little over a year. He was buried at Walton-on-Thames (where he had been nursed) on 28 March 1723. There would only be family sorrow at the almost unnoticed death of a small baby boy: Vanbrugh had felt as great a sadness a few months before at the death of his friend and patron, the Duke of Marlborough, and the subsequent refusal of the Duchess to let him design a 'magnificent & durable monument over him'.[65]

In the last four years of his life Vanbrugh continued actively with building at Seaton Delaval and Grimsthorpe. He was eating well: venison sent by the Duke of Newcastle, drinking 'rare good Cider' sent by Tonson, and commiserating with Hawksmoor who was laid up with gout. Various ailments did seize him,[66] and a 'distemper' got hold of him in September 1725. But within a month he was off 'upon a Northern Expedition' and swearing still at 'that B.B.B.B. Old B. the Dutchess of Marlb'. There were many things happening at Castle Howard, including the Temple, about which he wrote in his last recorded letter, 8 March 1726.[67] Some days later he developed a quinsy, a throat infection causing an abscess to form round the tonsils, making it difficult to breathe. On 26 March 1726, he died at his Whitehall house. At the end of the month the cortege bearing his body arrived at St Stephen Walbrook, a Wren city church and Sir John Vanbrugh Kt. was laid in the family vault in the north aisle.

Away at Stowe Lord Cobham reared the great pyramid[68] which had, according to Gilbert West, been Vanbrugh's last design. Long since demolished it bore over its door deep cut words, in Latin:

> Among the great number of buildings designed by Sir John Vanbrugh in these gardens, Cobham desired this pyramid to be sacred to his memory.

The London vault was walled over in the nineteenth century, and with no monument or inscription surviving, it is the 'heavy loads' of his buildings and the light fantasy of his several comedies which are the enduring monuments.

In life Sir John Vanbrugh may well have been more guileful, aggressive and resourceful[69] than several quotations about the wit and good nature of 'dear Van' suggest. But whatever the true measure of his personality his wife, just 33 years old at his death, stayed true to his memory through a long widowhood. She had to endure alone the sadness at the death in 1745 of their soldier-son Charles, fighting against the French at Fontenoy. Her own long life, spanning the reigns of five monarchs, came to an end in 1776, when she was in her 83rd year.

II

Great Fine Houses

. . . the expense of living in this Great fine house, do's not amount to above a hundred pounds a year, more than was spent in the old one.

Sir John Vanbrugh, writing of Castle Howard,
to James Craggs, senior, October 1713.

CASTLE HOWARD

On 25 December 1699, John Vanbrugh wrote to Lord Manchester, lately Ambassador in Venice, and then in Paris, that 'I have been this Summer at my Ld. Carlisle's, and Seen most of the great houses in the North ... There has been a great many Criticks consulted upon it [the plans] since, and no objection being made to't, the Stone is raising, and the Foundations will be laid in the Spring. The Modell is preparing in wood, wch when done, is to travel to Kensington where the King's thoughts upon't are to be had.'[1] Castle Howard, 15 miles from York, was built for the 3rd Earl of Carlisle (7) to replace the old castle of Henderskelfe, handed down to him in direct line by five generations of Howard ancestors. The chronicler, John Leland, visited it about 1540, and in terse appreciation noted that 'the park of Hinderskel to my estimation is a 4 miles yn cumpace, and hath much fair young wood yn it'. Elizabethan, Lord William Howard ('Belted Will', or 'Bald Willie' as he was irreverently called) acquired Henderskelfe through his marriage into the Dacre family; his wife's inheritance was in fact disputed, and not allowed until about 1600.[2] By this marriage the estates of Naworth in Cumberland, and Morpeth in Northumberland also came into his possession. His great-grandson Charles, although he was of Cromwell's Life Guards, and sat in the House of Lords, was after the Restoration created Earl of Carlisle by Charles II, in 1661. This Howard's son, the 2nd Earl, succeeded him in 1685, and died in 1692. His grandson, Charles the 3rd Earl, was then 23 years old, and was 30 in 1699, when he engaged Vanbrugh as his architect.[3]

Before setting the stage of Vanbrugh's first great achievement, and noting the important role there of Nicholas Hawksmoor, it is necessary to discuss the earlier designs prepared by William Talman (1650–1719).[4] For 14 years (1689–1702) Talman had been Comptroller of the King's Works, but at the death of William III in 1702 he was superseded by Vanbrugh, who had the support of his patron, Lord Carlisle, then Lord Treasurer.

Talman's reputation as an architect was considerable and his plans showed great flair; but his stock suffered because of the 'vexation and disappointment' caused his patrons by his choleric attitudes. In the volume of his drawings (now in the British Architectural Library) are two plans endorsed 'Designed for my Ld. Carlisle'. These show the centre block, and four rooms of varying shape on each front. In this design Talman was to collaborate (as on several occasions) with the formal garden designer, George London, and in one of the latter's northern journeys a grand plan was evolved for Castle Howard.[5]

It was here that dispute crept in; Talman had demanded a high price for his plans, which Lord Carlisle refused to pay. In an interesting letter of 15 June 1703 to the 1st Duke of Newcastle[6] (for whose house, Welbeck, Talman had also submitted plans) Vanbrugh revealed the rivalry existing between them. Subsequent events indicated that his triumphs were to be at Talman's expense, especially at Castle Howard.

The George London designs for Castle Howard came to light in 1951[7], among 16 drawings for Castle Howard (now in the Victoria & Albert Museum, London). These drawings fall into two categories, which Laurence Whistler has labelled the 'First' and 'Second' Proposals. The earliest drawings (**10**, **13**, **24**) show that there was much rearrangement to be done, before the full rich engravings in *Vitruvius Britannicus* (1717) (**8**) could reflect a truer idea of the 'Great fine house' Vanbrugh had referred to in his letter to James Craggs.[8] In these early plans the kitchen and stable courts do not appear, and whilst the experienced touch of Hawksmoor may be discerned – with all the details and careful designs being made to his instructions – it did not intrude enough to distort Vanbrugh's ideas. Vanbrugh, like Wren, found Hawksmoor an invaluable partner, and collaborated with him fully at Castle Howard. The slightly older man (Hawksmoor was born in 1661, three years before Vanbrugh) had a capacity for detail and a greater knowledge at this early stage. Vanbrugh had yet to entirely abandon his military career, and was involved in the heady mechanics of writing for the stage. Hawksmoor was therefore needed to ease Vanbrugh's principal contribution to English architecture – a 'Baroque variant' of what was available on the Continent, and engraved in several published works (**20**, **21**).

In the second group of proposals big changes were indicated. The revised plan (**17**) shows the area near the hall being prepared for the reception of a heavy lantern; the kitchen wing has been detached, and connected to the house by a corridor. With this plan Vanbrugh finally overcame the attempts of William Talman to be Lord Carlisle's architect. The high cupola is, however, still absent from the second proposals (**14**) – it was not built until 1706, as noted below. In the first and second plans (**10**, **17**) Vanbrugh designed a house with square ends. Early in 1705, when working on plans for Blenheim, he incorporated terminal bow-windows there; and after inserting one (not built) for the east end at Castle Howard, he went on to use the idea at least 17 times in various houses. Such a bow was used at the west end of Castle Howard in 1706 – it can be seen in the perspective view in *Vitruvius Britannicus* (**8**), but was swept away in the creation of that wing by Sir Thomas Robinson 50 years later (**25**).

The extensive archives at Castle Howard have only yielded one Vanbrugh letter and two from Hawksmoor, written within the main years of building activity before 1720. Vanbrugh's letter, written in 1700[9], was concerned with the provision of a suitable labour force, and with the opinions of 'Mr Hawksmoor'. He hoped the master craftsmen, the mason and carpenter, would agree to the acceptance of terms much lower than they were accustomed to receive in London, and feared that in consequence the work would suffer in quality: 'So this would give 'em a loophole to play the Rogue very much ...'. The names of these two master craftsmen are not recorded; it has been assumed that the leading men employed by Wren – Edward Strong and John Longland – were used, their previous work being known to Hawksmoor. When negotiations with London craftsmen fell through they turned to the capable men in the nearby city of York. Hawksmoor wrote to Lord Carlisle on 26 May 1701 to report; 'I find the work at Henderscelfe to go on with vigour and gt. industrie ...'. Work started with 'Ignorant Masons at Lower Rates' and the first payment in 1701 was £200 to William Smith 'upon acct. of himself & partns who hath obliged themselves to Build a new house at Henders Kelfe.' William Smith dropped out at a later date, but his companions, John Ellsworth and Manger (sometimes 'Major') Smith, were employed until 1719.

Work started in the East Kitchen Wing and by 1703 this was complete, with a corridor connecting it to the house. As the men moved westwards across the site, digging out foundations, and then erecting the dressed blocks of stone, cut from a quarry in the park, Vanbrugh's thoughts and Hawksmoor's pencil were directed to the facades of the main block (**13**, **16**) and its surmounting cupola. The sources an architect uses to arrive at such decisions are one of the most fascinating aspects of any commission. Hawksmoor was a master of the English Baroque 'more assured in his command of the classical vocabulary than the untrained Vanbrugh, more imaginative in his vision than the intellectual Wren'.[10] He had studied all there was to see in Italy and France (and medieval England) but only through his extensive library of books and engravings.[11] He had not travelled abroad, but he had taken to heart the advice given by John Evelyn in *Sculptura* (1662) that the use of engravings helped in understanding the arts, and in spreading knowledge about original works too expensive for many to acquire. Vanbrugh, of course, may have seen many actual buildings on his travels in France: still less do we know what books he possessed beyond a handful of titles, which are either mentioned in his letters or his account-book.

If there was novelty in the Castle Howard plan, it was the elevations which were more noticeable. French architectural books seem to have been studied, particularly Jean Marot's *L'Architecture française* (Paris, 1652) for such a design as the Electoral palace at Mannheim (**21**). Pérelle's engraving of Louis XIV's (now vanished) Château de Marly (**20**) may have been the inspiration for the giant Corinthian Order which characterizes the south front. Certainly the appearance of William Talman's Chatsworth, which Vanbrugh told Lord Manchester he had seen in 1699[12], and Hawksmoor's own Easton Neston (1702), were influential sources on which to base any improvements. The accomplished layout of the plan (**18-19**) shows they tried hard to succeed, and please Lord Carlisle.

Vanbrugh wanted a centre block which would be joined to the wings by quadrants, and Hawksmoor added a note about these curved arcades or 'corridors' on one of the early 'revised' drawings (**16**). This block was to contain the great hall, and the final position of the stairs occupied them for a time in 1705, as the building reared up, and took on shape. The stairs were hidden at either side of the hall, and allowed dramatic shafting views through arches (**34**) of the dark voids, and the massive piers supporting the painted dome (**33**). At the back of the hall was a Saloon, with state rooms to either side, connected by a corridor which ran the whole length of the wings (**32**) across the south front. This can be seen on the 'General Plan' (**18**) and gave some privacy to each room, unlike Wren's Hampton Court, and Chatsworth, where rooms succeed one another, connected only by doors admitting to the total space of each.

On the north side the central block was flanked by two wings reaching forward (**11**) and containing the kitchen (east), and the chapel (west). The side courts projected out behind them seem to have followed in date those at Blenheim, but we know that whilst they are depicted in *Vitruvius Britannicus* (**8**) the court to the west was not built. The engraving also shows what Sir Thomas Robinson spoiled by the rebuilding at the west end in the 1750s – the whole panoply of the entrance forecourt. The small domes were intended to complement the central dominant cupola, and the whole dramatic silhouette, topped with urns and statues, was to be approached through a giant gateway, flanked by four obelisks.

At Blenheim most of the external stonework was done by Grinling Gibbons and his assistants, who had a workshop on the site. At Castle Howard Samuel Carpenter, a York mason, and the Huguenot refugee carver, Nadauld, together with 'Mr Sabyn, Joyner', worked in wood and stone. Carpenter busied himself in 'the Drawing Roome Next the Main Pile' and also in 'My Lord's Grand Cabinett' where he carved '125 Cartozzas' (cartouches?). He embellished the south front with stone drapery

(**26**) charging 50s. each for the '27 Pilaster Capitalls of the Corinthian Order'. These included those of the central block, where also for 50s., he had carved 'A Shield and Cherabin head over the window', which we recognize as the keystone of the upper central window (**27**).

For the same sort of work, and in the same year (1705), the accounts show a payment to 'Mr Nedos' (Nadauld) of £137. 2s. 7d. Nadauld worked at Chatsworth as well as Castle Howard, and had a special shed put up for his use. He worked in wood in the Grand Cabinet, and in his 'Lordship's Apartment', and carved in stone on the south front (as at Chatsworth) the tritons and lions on the great cornice (**27**). The four figures in niches which flank the main entrance on the north side (**11**) are also his work, and he toiled at enriching the cupola (1706), and the keystones of the Hall until 1710.

Inside, several chimney pieces were provided by William Harvey, who made them of 'deal carved about'. The fine Baroque chimneypiece in the Hall was handed over to the care of the Italian stuccoists Giovanni Bagutti and Giuseppe Plura.[13] It complemented the colourful decorative paintings by Giovanni Antonio Pellegrini and Marco Ricci far overhead (**33-34**) with its froth of white stucco.

Pellegrini had come to England, with Marco Ricci, under the patronage of Lord Manchester and was at Castle Howard by 1709. He was later to move to Kimbolton to work (under Vanbrugh) for the same patron who had helped his introduction to England, Lord Manchester. Some loose accounts among the 'Building Bills' at Castle Howard show this date, when it was 'Agre'd with Mr Pelegrini for ye painting at Castle Howard, to give him £800.' The final quittance for £852. 5s. was signed in September 1712. Some of Pellegrini's work was unfortunately destroyed in the fire of November 1940, but was illustrated in 1928.[14] Marco Ricci worked in addition in the Garden Hall (also destroyed), receiving two payments of £20 each in November 1709.

The complex iconographic programme of the painted and sculptural decoration in the house has received some scholarly attention in recent years[15], and is summarized here. The dome painting (**62**) represents the legend of Phaeton, who, after being given permission by Apollo to drive the chariot of the sun, fell to earth. It has been assumed that Lord Carlisle would not wish to remind visitors entering his 'Great fine house' that he had fallen from high political office, being turned out from his office as First Lord of the Treasury by Queen Anne. Furthermore Apollo was equated with the magnificence and temporal power of Louis XIV, the 'Sun King', an enemy, whose forces the Duke of Marlborough had defeated but recently. Rather would it seem that the eight sculptures on the parapet, now much worn, but representing the four Vestal Virgins, together with representations of Socrates, Plato, Cicero and Seneca, were combined with the paintings to tell another story. The legend of Phaeton, before having an allegorical significance attached to it, was a myth about creation. On entering Castle Howard one was therefore faced with a cosmology – the creation of a universe – of 'continents, elements, music and the firmament', and paintings betokening 'time, change, metamorphosis and the fall'.

Furthermore, in the Grand Cabinet at the west end of the garden front (destroyed by Sir Thomas Robinson) the cosmology embraced Diana and Endymion as a further part of Pellegrini's painted story. Endymion lay asleep on Mount Latmos, and the moon goddess, Diana, fell in love with him. Through their association for a single night Jupiter condemned Endymion to perpetual sleep. In the Hall then was Phaeton, racing through the panoply of the heavens in his high chariot behind the four prancing horses of the sun, and at the end of the west wing there was the quiet depiction of Diana and Endymion, representing night, sleep and the moon. The giant order of the piers and the painted dome above were, in one splendid gesture – worthy to be a stage-set by Ferdinando Bibiena for the Habsburgs in Vienna – but stating to all, the grand and theatrical effect which Vanbrugh had achieved throughout this, his first commission, for the erstwhile Lord High Treasurer (**7**).

With the main house erected, the outbuildings and entrances (**31**) were next in line to be assembled, but not without some difficulty. At some point it had been resolved to add office courts to the original house, with two forecourt wings. Until they were built the buildings of old Henderskelfe Castle served. The building of the kitchen court, for example, occupied many years, and its progress is not easy to trace in the surviving accounts. The Great Obelisk Gate (**7**), too, receives mysterious mention in the accounts for 1718. But in Vanbrugh's letters of 1724 the question is still in abeyance as to whether there should be a central gateway at all. Vanbrugh by this time was hoping to persuade Lord Carlisle to a more important move, to begin the west wing, and on 21 November 1724 he wrote to Lord Carlisle: 'As much as I love a Gateway, and by consequence Shou'd be glad to See one up at Castle Howard; I must own, I think the Wing of so much more weight to the Credit of the House . . .'.[16] In the following month he argued against the gateway (at Blenheim he argued the other way), and whilst after his death a low gate was built, which Hawksmoor did not think sufficiently dignified, it seems to have been a feature of the house which gave some considerable trouble.

In 1738 the 3rd Earl of Carlisle died. The various draft wills he had made from the 1720s carried bequests to Vanbrugh, Hawksmoor and the clerk of works, William Etty, and were perhaps a touching vindication of them in the light of what the Burlingtonians were to do at the house and mausoleum in later years.[17] There seems no reason to disbelieve the story told by John, 5th Duke of Rutland, who as a youth in 1796 visited Castle Howard and three years later married the then Earl's daughter. He stated that Robinson had meant to replace much of Vanbrugh's work by his own. However, the death of the 4th Earl in 1758, five years after Robinson's west wing was begun, and the heavy gambling debts incurred by the 5th Earl, in company with his friend, Charles James Fox, prevented the east wing being replaced. The proportions of the front (**25**) were of course not too satisfactory, but Robinson's elongations would have upset things still more; Horace Walpole said that when Vanbrugh and the youthful Robinson met once at Castle Howard they stood 'spitting and swearing at one another'. From 1701 to 1737 it cost the 3rd Earl, finally, some £78,000[18] to erect his house. Vanbrugh, however, had long since turned his attention to a great pile which was to cost almost four times as much[19], Blenheim Palace.

BLENHEIM PALACE

It would seem likely that it was Lord Carlisle's influence which had secured for Vanbrugh the post of Comptroller of Works in 1702, but the commission for Blenheim (1705) was another matter. In June 1704 the 1st Duke of Marlborough's forces had joined with those of Prince Eugene of Savoy, and Prince Louis of Baden, in attacking Schellenberg, the Bavarian fortress. They then moved into position in early August 1704 along the banks of Danube, to face the 28 regiments of Louis XIV's army, gathered between Höckstadt and Blenheim, under the direction of Maréchal Tallard. As the battle of Blenheim (13 August) neared its close the victorious Duke despatched Colonel Daniel Parke on his eight-day journey across Europe with the famous message, informing his Duchess and his Queen (Sarah sent Parke on from St James's to Windsor) that: '... her army has had a glorious victory', and that Tallard was his prisoner.

Four weeks later, on 7 September 1704, the Queen and the Duchess drove together 'in a rich coach with eight horses' to a thanksgiving service in St Paul's Cathedral: the battle of Blenheim had shaken the world, and made it 'look upon the Duke of Marlborough with a sort of amazement, as upon one destined by Providence to rescue and establish the Liberties of Europe'.[20] Crown and Parliament were soon to vie with each other in offering their victorious general a generous reward, but, alas, bitterness was to grow slowly in intensity between the Queen and the Duchess, or 'Mrs Morley' and 'Mrs Freeman', as they had elected to call themselves, in order that they could 'converse as Equals'. The appropriate gift seemed to the Queen to be that of the royal estate at Woodstock in Oxfordshire, with its ruined manor (**38**) as the site of a great mansion she would have built for the Duke. It was perhaps with this in mind that Sarah had, after a stormy personal campaign, obtained the post of Cofferer to the Household for Francis, 2nd Earl of Godolphin, who had married her daughter, Henrietta. In June 1705 Lord Treasurer Godolphin 'at the request and desire of the said Duke of Marlborough' signed a warrant on 9 June 1705, appointing John Vanbrugh Surveyor of all the works and buildings which the duke had 'resolv'd to erect' at Woodstock, and authorizing him to make and sign contracts 'for and on behalf of the said Duke'. Sarah's opinion of the architect was that she had heard of him as a writer of comedies but she had not yet met him. She wrote later one of her irascible commentaries on the start of it all:

> At the beginning of those works I never had spoake to him, but as soon as I knew & saw the maddnesse of the whole Design I opposed it all that was possible for me to doe ... I don't know that the Queen had any particular favour for Sir C. Wren, tho hee had been an old servant, but 'tis certain that old Craggs[21], who was as ill a man as ever I knew recommended Sr John Vanbrugh to the Duke of Marl....[22]

But, for the moment, Vanbrugh was her witty, engaging companion and someone to be teased about Swift's verse on his Goose-Pie house in Whitehall (3). There was, however, the wider problem of the wording of the Warrant to occupy her. It contained no mention of the Crown, or the Queen 'whose present the palace was reputed to be',[23] and by now the site had been chosen by the Duke and Vanbrugh and the design and model[24] approved. On Monday, 18 June 1705, at six in the evening, the foundation-stone itself was laid. Vanbrugh, along with six others[25], struck the polished stone with a hammer, and they each then cast a guinea beneath it. The stone, bearing the legend: 'In memory of the battel of Blenheim, June 18, 1705, Anna Regina' was lowered into position beneath the intended site of the Bow-Window Room on the east front (**58**). The Duke, absent abroad on his next campaign, was delighted with the prospect of so great a present, and the whole of the surrounding part of Oxfordshire danced and drank the night away on the chosen site, above the south bank of the Glyme brook. In the shadows on the north side lay the old manor house (**38**) where, tradition had it, Henry II came to visit his fair Rosamund. Yet, by the very show and vanity of the plans, there was sown in the Duchess's mind 'the seed of a future crop of nettles'. 'I made Mr Vanbrugh my enemy' she wrote later 'by the constant disputes I had with him to prevent his extravagance.'

At the start of the Blenheim works in the early summer of 1705 these thoughts were not yet active. Four or five quarries had been opened up in the park, but as the stone proved unsuitable (except for inside walls) Vanbrugh had to look elsewhere. He told the Duke that 'the number of Workmen on the House (besides the Gardens) will in a few days rise to near a Thousand', and by August 1705 it was 'near fifteen hundred'. These numbers excluded the stone carters who were bringing stone in from Sir Thomas Wheate's quarry at Glympton, and Lord Rochester's at Cornbury. Soon there would be need to look further afield to Kempster and Strong's quarries at Burford and Taynton, and to those at Barrington and Sherborne.[26] All 22 quarries were within a radius of 20 miles, and were visited regularly (1705–11) by Henry Joynes, the careful Blenheim Comptroller. In addition, stone for special purposes was obtained from Portland, Plymouth and Ross-on-Wye. Together with all the other multifarious supplies it came by the carters' teams or by West Country barges to Abingdon, and then by road to the site.

The whole conception of Blenheim was on a monumental scale, and was accounted for in Vanbrugh's letter of 30 September 1710 to Lord Poulett:[27]

> When the Queen had declared she would build a House in Woodstock parke for the Duke of Marlborough, and that she mean't it in Memory of the Great Services he had done her and the Nation, I found it the Opinion of all people & of all partys I convers'd with, that altho the building was to be calculat'd for, and Adapted to, a private Habitation, Yet it ought at ye same time, to be consider'd as both a Royall and a National Monument, and care taken in the design, and the Execution, that it might have ye Qualitys proper to such a Monument, Vizt. Beauty, Magnificence and Duration. . . .

A national monument, then, and secondly, a house for family life, yet still with something of Castle Howard about its disposition. Both are entered on the north side, and have a hall, saloon, state rooms on the south, and staircases adjacent to either side of the hall (plans, **18–19**, **40–41**). The family rooms, as at Castle Howard, were put behind the east facades, but the whole of the west front was occupied by the Gallery (now Long Library). There are of course differences in overall size, and in the mass and height of the central block, with the great portico rising to a pediment, fronting a yet higher one. There is a greater rhythmic pattern to the clustering of pilasters and columns, projections and recessions, to give the semi-Cyclopean effect, which in various forms was to characterize Vanbrugh's later work at Kimbolton and Seaton Delaval. Indeed Sir John Summerson has written[28] splendidly of the overwhelming effect of the north front:

> Look at the giant drama of the entrance court, the whole composed in a series of brief, potent assaults, each driving exactly to its objective and then halting, sharp. Every component is brief – the stretches of colonnade, the visible lengths of main facade, the emergent angles of the towers. And as if this brevity might be construed as weakness, each stop is double-stopped. Sentinel columns stand forward in pairs every time the colonnade of the courtyard halts. It is not enough for the portico to march out from the main pilastered front – the front itself must first step back. Even then, the portico doubles its outer columns and squares them both into piers – monstrous over-emphasis indeed, but that the piers have another duty and must slide upwards through the entablature to prop the twin beginnings of a second pediment – those separated fragments

which are the last things one remembers of Blenheim and which leave a hint of doom, like the crag of an antique ruin.

The teams of craftsmen had been assembled carefully. Mindful that those at Castle Howard could, if hired too casually, 'play the Rogue very much', Vanbrugh had asked 'a great variety of the Workmen of the same Trade in different Countrys [that is, counties of England] and quite unacquainted with one another, for their Proposals.' When these were received the work was divided between many undertakers of each trade, 'with different Rates according to the Performance expected from them.' Edward Strong, father and son, well-known to Sir Christopher Wren for their work at St Paul's Cathedral, were the principal masons (they also part-owned the stone quarries being used at Barrington and Taynton). They were joined by the Oxford mason-partners, John Townesend and Bartholomew Peisley, with Henry Banks (or Banckes) as the fifth mason-quarry owner.

To this core of experienced men were added the 'specialists of even higher accomplishment' – Grinling Gibbons and his team, for most of the stone decoration, Sir James Thornhill, and Louis Laguerre (ironically the godson of Louis XIV, whose armies the Duke had vanquished) as painters, Robert Wetherill and Isaac Mansfield as plasterers, the Hopsons and Smallwells as joiners, Matthew Banks and John Barton as carpenters, and clock makers, sun-dial makers and a whole host of other talents were assembled. All their names were entered with regularity into the vast ledgers kept by Henry Joynes, his clerk Jefferson, and (from September 1708), the other Blenheim Comptroller, Tilleman Bobart. Payment to them, nevertheless, was to become another – and vexatious – matter, but the building still carried up, high above the great earth piles that Henry Wise's garden teams were digging out on the north side for the causeway and the foundations of the bridge. Checking everything at the drawing board was the watchful Nicholas Hawksmoor, seeing all was well.

No calculations of the time to be taken in building had been given to the absent Duke, or to the brooding watchful Duchess. If she walked the site – as she surely did – from the lifting of the first grass she would have seen the thousands of cubic yards of earth and clay that Wise's teams were carting away, as well as his great preparations for gardens and parterres. Henry Wise (1653-1738)[29] had been gardener to both William III and Queen Anne, and knew from experience, that if (with Charles Bridgeman's help) he set out a plan of great avenues (**42**), parterres and gravel walks it could all be accomplished. Within 18 months of the laying of the foundation-stone, the north and east elm avenues were planted, and shrubs and flowers were being sent down from his Brompton nursery. But on another of the Duchess's walks she might well have felt horrified to see that, as well as alterations in the agreed placing of the Chapel and Kitchen, two years into building the intended Doric south front, then 8 metres (27 feet) high, was being pulled down to be rebuilt using the Corinthian order.

The whole frontispiece (**56**), which was given, finally, its great surmounting bust of Louis XIV, thus needed to be given more height. The great arcaded lanterns, after endless site discussions, and the viewing of cut-outs *in situ*, were pushed up even more to achieve the desired silhouette. The overall affect achieved can best be judged from the Doric elevation (**54**) and a view of the south front itself (**55**). Had it all come to the architect's mind as he visited Holland in the summer of 1706, perhaps seeing buildings like the Huis ten Bosch at the Hague, or leafing through his Palladio or the engravings of ideal châteaux (**45**) in Le Pautre's *OEuvres d'Architecture*? In any case, he was deviating from the wooden model, approved by the Queen, and telling few about it. Not to be outdone, the Duchess, who had also noted that the Duke had ordered alterations to the basement windows of the garden front, told the Strongs to pull down the west bow window then up almost 4 metres (13 ft), and rebuilt it to admit more light. They could neither win nor lose. They could record the amendments in their bills and hope to be paid, they could even put up with taking down their good masonry, but what did they think of the Duchess then urging their Comptroller Henry Joynes that 'My lord Marl says his life will not bee long enough to enjoy much of the hous if it is not carry'd up as fast as it can bee'?[30] Inevitably there was frustration, exacerbated by the constant shortage of money. 'There is So much money requir'd for Publick good this Year', Vanbrugh wrote on 18 July 1707, to Lord Manchester, 'that my Ld Treasurer can't Afford us at Blenheim half what we want; however, there will a great deal be done; And two Summers more will finish it.' For the moment the 'Lady Dutchess' expressed herself as entirely pleased and, Vanbrugh continued: 'she found She shou'd live to Ask my pardon, for ever having Quarrell'd with me.'[31]

If the Duchess, for the moment only, did not quarrel with Vanbrugh, she expressed almost daily disagreement over several more years with everything else about the great house. She disliked the schemes for the decoration of the entrance hall and Saloon (**60-61**) and that for the Saloon was also roundly condemned in 16 pages of 'vigorous French' by a painter, Louis Silvestre. He disliked the niches (**61**), but these survived until the Duchess called in Laguerre as her painter to supplant Thornhill and give her a painted scheme of which she at least approved. Away in the distance on the north side there was also the partly finished Grand Bridge (**66-67**) which she had never accepted as necessary. Stone was in short supply, and almost as the still ebullient Vanbrugh was writing to Lord Manchester (his patron at Kimbolton) on 16 March 1707/8 that

Blenheim was much advanced, 'And one Summer more I hope will Cover it all', the ever-slow trickle of Treasury money almost ceased entirely. The sum of £3000 was sent, but to cover the cost of preparing flower gardens in the shortest, wettest part of the year, roofing the stables and kitchen wings, and Gibbons's first bill for stone-carving this did not amount to much. The Duchess was, however, soon to be laying a foundation-stone of her own, that of Marlborough House in London, supervised by Sir Christopher Wren (and his son) of the old guard, but one of great talent and held in 'great tenderness' by the Duke's lively architect. She was to be advised against building it by the Duke, but it was a house that, to her could be made much more habitable than the cold Baroque voids of a still unroofed Blenheim, and that was reason enough.

The Duke meanwhile was also well occupied – thrusting at the head of his armies on across Europe, the battle of Oudenarde, the capitulation of Lille, Ghent and Bruges, the forcing of the Scheldt, the siege of Tournai, and the Battle of Malplaquet within his roll-call. And yet, in a brief respite, and during the great frost of January–April 1709, the Duke still found opportunity to visit England, and to come to see the hard, white, rearing expanses of his Royal 'present'. A month later, having announced to his excited architect that it looked good, he was back at the front, and the Duchess, in London, laid the foundation-stone of Marlborough House.

As Vanbrugh's visits to the great works at Blenheim were carried out in both winter and summer, and sometimes of long duration, he had often eyed the old Manor House as a suitable place in which to stay. He therefore ordered the least ruined parts to be repaired, and was pleased to be told, as he wrote in March 1708, that the 'Roof is up'.[32] The Duchess, despite her vigilance, had no knowledge of these reparations, having intended that the whole of it should be swept away. She further accused Vanbrugh of squandering public money for his own convenience, and whilst he protested about the alleged amount to Lord Godolphin, he had to compile a memorandum on 11 June 1709 to defend himself.[33] He remarked in it on the value of the remains of distant times, on the reasons for their erection, and continued with 'Other Considerations' to assist the historical argument. These concentrated on the need for 'Variety of Objects' on the north side of the house which, rightly disposed, would 'indeed supply all the wants of Nature in that Place'. The Duchess appended a note to Vanbrugh's earlier letter about the ruin (31 May 1709):[34] 'All that Sir J.V. says in this letter is false . . .'.

No quarter, however, was given. Vanbrugh for his part wrote loftily, and almost as an afterthought, that the Duke had known of the matter, and that he was preparing a sketch which would serve 'much better than A thousand words' to explain the delights of the old Manor to them both. He denied that he wanted merely to live in 'so poor a contrivance for so worthless a thing', but that it needed saving for 'the Beauty of the Fabrick'. Despite the memorandum, his letters and the sketch, the Duchess directed him otherwise and Vanbrugh reported, perhaps reluctantly, on 9 June 1709[35], that when he was last at Blenheim, 'I set Men on to take down the Ruins at the Old Manor as was directed', but that he was leaving the 'Chappel last, because I was preparing a little Picture of what had been in general propos'd to be done with the Descent from the Avenue to the Bridge ...'. The Duchess can hardly have been pleased at further mention of the Bridge, which she still thought was a great extravagance, but perhaps, she mused, the stone from the Manor could help build it? She little realized either that her architect was playing for time, for the Marlboroughs were now finding less favour with the Queen – or that the day would come, in 1713, when the architect would live in the manor, for a time and in their absence abroad in exile. Whilst work on the main house had proceeded throughout 1709, and the first half of 1710, the contractors were becoming uneasy over extending credit after the dismissal in August 1710 of Lord Godolphin as Treasurer. The Queen was often quoted as expressing herself in the terms 'O, that my Lord Godolphin would be parted from the Duchess of Marlborough', and now, finally, she had dismissed him, with 'a pension of four thousand a year, and I desire that, instead of bringing the staff to me, you will break it, which I believe will be easier to us both.'[36]

The break of a different kind – with Sarah, Duchess of Marlborough – came just as sharply later in the same year, although again the Queen did not find herself in an easy position. The Duke was still leading her armies in successful victories, but Sarah had become too reckless in her accusations. She was threatening to publish their letters, and charging the Queen with very grave matters such as lesbianism with Abigail Hill (Lady Masham) who had supplanted her in royal favour. Sarah had, perhaps wisely, stopped all work at Blenheim a month or two before (October 1710), with £7000 allowed for the work to be covered for the winter.

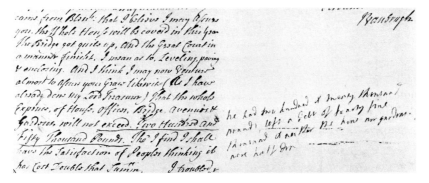

Part of a Letter, Sir John Vanbrugh to 1st Duchess of Marlborough, 6 June 1710. (Photograph: courtesy David Green, from his *Blenheim Palace* (1951) pl. 24).

43

The snow settled on the great house in December and the final break with the Queen was now a painful fact for all to witness. The Duke was also finding out too many hard truths, and realizing that 'a man must bear with a good deal, to be quiet at home'.[37] And bear even more, when the home he had been promised was 'quiet' through delays in building it, brought on in large measure by his own whirlwind of a wife. The friendship between the Queen and Duchess had lasted 30 years, but in the final sad debacle the Duchess had removed angrily all the portable fittings from her apartments at St James's, and the Queen had ordered the building of Blenheim to halt, saying 'that she would not build the Duke a house when the Duchess was pulling her's to pieces.'[38]

Such were the reasons for the hold-ups in work at Blenheim, even ignoring the gradual wind-down in the supply of money which had preceded the rift between Duchess and Queen. Now, the Duchess, with her own convenient house in London, thought Blenheim would never be finished: in any case, she wrote, 'it could never be any advantage or pleasure to my Lord Marlborough or his Family, but might remain as a Moniment of Ingratitude, instead of what was once intended'.[39] She reckoned, however, without some of the loyalty the Crown owed to the Duke, and the Duke's acumen in approaching the new Lord Treasurer, Robert Harley, Earl of Oxford for a continuation of funds. Whilst an order was given for the payment of £20,000, none of it reached Blenheim before August. There, all was still disorder, frowned down on by the still-incomplete, gaunt structure of the Bridge, and with disgruntled craftsmen, already over-stretched by extending credit: the debt to the Strongs as masons was, for example, – still unpaid – over £6000, with a further £3000 for stone and carriage.

The Blenheim building programme, with its insatiable need for Government finance, was an awkward venture to control. In addition, the Duke for whom it was intended was now the object of a steady campaign of intrigue, instituted by Lord Treasurer Oxford. He alleged great irregularity in the Duke's military accounts, and as the Duke himself had refused the Queen's invitation to resume his place in the Cabinet, and to stop opposing the proposals for the Peace of Utrecht, he had laid himself open to serious charges. Soon the Blenheim workforce faced worries beyond its immediate concern with winter weather and the lack of payment for their arduous work; what little money they had in any case was soon to be dispersed at Christmas. When they returned to the frozen site it was to learn, on 29 December 1711, that the Queen had dismissed the man who was her Captain-General and their immediate patron. The Queen might well squirm at his precise and sharp rejoinder, written on New Year's Day (from his St Albans estate of Holywell)[40] but even she found it difficult to halt the ponderous machine of the Treasury and payments for

Blenheim trickled on for another few months until June. Gibbons and his assistants were among the last to lay down their work, and all of them might be able to take some payment from what came, but, as with the work, the arrears were left unheeded.

The scaffolding at the house was now struck, in anticipation of the visit by the Duke. He came when the sun was high, in August, ready to talk with Vanbrugh and all the country gentlemen who awaited him, and to urge at his departure that Henry Joynes should care well for the gaunt shell of his house.

The site was soon the quiet haven of the gardeners and the night watchmen; the Duke went abroad into self-imposed exile in December 1712, and was joined two months later by the Duchess. Vanbrugh for his part was turning his thoughts to moving into the old Manor, which he had prevented from being destroyed by the simple expedient of ignoring all orders to carry out the job. A pastoral phase in his relationship to Blenheim was long overdue, and there was also now time to do such minor tasks as writing a letter (on 25 January 1713) about paving the town of Woodstock. This prosaic matter was calculated however to echo far beyond those flagstones, as we have noted earlier, and to lose him his comptrollership, and election as Garter King of Arms.

'That now she has done with me': this was how Vanbrugh described the Queen's attitude in a letter of 29 May 1714 to the Duke of Marlborough, who was still abroad with the Duchess. The Duke had asked for 'an account of what the buildings &c at Blenheim had cost; what was owing, and what might be required to finish the design?'[41] The Duke could consider returning for he had presumably received intelligence that the Queen had been taken ill the previous December, had continued so throughout January 1714, and that her 'days were numbered, limited to months, if not to weeks'.[42] Vanbrugh gave the Duke in the same letter of 29 May 1714 a full account:

> By the memorial I gave in to the Lord Treasurer the 15th of June 1711. The Demand to clear the Debts, and to finish what was always supposed the Queen intended to do; was £87,000 of which there has since been issued from the Treasury, 20,000£. The Debts now are about 42,000£. So that according to that demand; were the Debts paid, there wou'd remain £25,000 to finish Building. And I am truly of opinion there wou'd not then rest anything considerable upon your Grace to do, as the design now stands: Tho many things no doubt might be proposed for farther improvement of the Seat, but very little wou'd be necessary.
>
> The whole sum that has been received from the Treasury, is 220,000£. So that the whole sum of Money issued, Debts owing and what has been asked from the Queen, amounts to £287,000. A large Sum for a house, but a poor reward for the services that occasioned the Building it. . . .

The Duke was already mindful that he had been sued in November 1713 in his absence for £350 owing on Blenheim work to the joiner Robert Barker, and that Vanbrugh was telling him, also in the letter of 29 May 1714, that he was trying to prevent the Strong family of masons from doing the same. A change in all their fortunes was needed, and might still come from the Queen. She was beset with alternate bouts of illness and fevered activity, and while preoccupied with the Protestant Succession, the divisions between Whig and Tory, Jacobite and Hanoverian, had never really lost contact with her former captain-general. The Lords Sunderland and Godolphin were now dead, and Lord Treasurer Oxford had been discredited by the coalition of forces led by Lord Bolingbroke. The Queen needed the support of Marlborough, and through the offices of a number of his close friends, General William Cadogan, and perhaps Bolingbroke and the elder James Craggs, the Duke (and his wife) were asked to return to England. They would come in the knowledge that the Duke had been promised the restoration of all his offices.

As Lord Oxford surrendered his white staff to the Queen on 27 July 1714 after her spirited dismissal of him, he warned her never to trust Marlborough, 'who was returning to England only to betray her and cause civil unrest.'[43] Over the next few days however the Queen's illness took its toll: she weakened, and slipped into insensibility to all events around her. Early on the morning of Sunday, 1 August 1714 Queen Anne died at Kensington Palace. The Marboroughs, tossed in the Channel by adverse winds, landed at Dover the afternoon of the same day, and arriving in London were greeted with joyous acclaim by the noisy excited crowds. The Queen's body was not laid to rest until 23 August in the presence of all the silver-caned élite, including two of the Duke and Duchess of Marlborough's daughters, Henrietta, Countesss of Godolphin, and Mary, Duchess of Montagu.

After the September accession of George I as King, Marlborough, who had been momentarily irritated that he had not been appointed as a regent following the Queen's death, was restored to all his offices. Presumably at Marlborough's intervention, the King also dubbed Vanbrugh as a knight on 19 September 1714, the first in his reign. 'Sir John Vanbrugh' was then invited by Lord Halifax, the new First Lord of the Treasury, to make suggestions for the reorganization of the Office of Works. Four months after his knighthood, on 24 January 1715 Vanbrugh was restored to his post as Comptroller of Works. He had waited too long, in an active career, for restitution.

At Blenheim most of the main building had been covered by 1712, and now, with a new King, the outstanding problems left at the cessation of work by the Queen and the Duchess's intervention could perhaps be resolved. The Strongs were still reluctant to be dissuaded from sueing

Marlborough: he was sure the Crown would repay all debts in full, and asked Vanbrugh for another estimate. The finishing of Blenheim, 'Offices, Bridge, and Out Walls, of Courts and Gardens', Vanbrugh wrote somewhat later, would amount to £54,000. His letter to the Duke does not survive: these facts appear in one he sent to Lord Carlisle in June 1717[44], and are referred to in a further one to the Duke of 27 June 1717. This was endorsed by the Duchess, now very active again, in deed and in word:

> Lord Carlisle carryd a most infamous letter of Sr Johns writing to him which was contrived between them, to make the Duke of Marl. uneasy with me, full of nothing but falsehoods only because I would not let Sr John do all the rediculous things imaginable at Blenheim & mend his fortune.[45]

Several hundred persons were owed money, and Henry Joynes laboured at his accounts, which were to be considered by the appointed commissioners headed by William Lowndes, the Secretary to the Treasury. By ponderous form the Debt was acknowledged, and adjusted in a way Parliament would approve – paying £16,000, or a little over a third of the £45,000 Joynes had totalled was due. Vanbrugh, owed £2463, received, as with the rest, less than a third, a mere £800. Everyone was expected, after a long delay of four years when they had hardly seen the Duke and Vanbrugh, and with the death of the Queen extending their worry, to take up their tools and sharpen up the mossy edges of the standing stones. The older masons, the Strongs and Banks, refused and prepared for litigation; but their foremen, Christopher 'Kit' Cash and Joshua Fletcher, anxious to prove their ability and willing for lower rates, stepped in.

The long strain of foreign campaign and the death of his second daughter Anne in April 1716 had taken its toll on the Duke. On 28 May 1716 he suffered a stroke, from which he partially recovered, but it was followed in November, by a second. Accordingly, Vanbrugh found himself dealing with the Duchess, and not least because she asked him to play matchmaker in bringing his friend Thomas, Duke of Newcastle to court her grand-daughter Harriet.[46] He set about this enjoyable task with characteristic aplomb, but it was typical of the Duchess to resent the act afterwards, and to try and hasten the ever-difficult process of bringing a plain young woman to a worldly man by hiring a professional matchmaker. It showed her ever-mounting desire to be rid of Vanbrugh, and it became one of the main causes of the final rupture between them. Furthermore the Duchess was also at work on drawing up all the detailed accusations against Vanbrugh, 'from the time Blenheim was first ordered by the Queen ...'.[47] Her own Marlborough House had been finished in two years: here at Blenheim, after over ten years, their own apartments in the east wing were still not habitable. She and the Duke had moved from taking the waters at Bath to Blenheim, to put up at High

Lodge, and from there she could gaze, and foment in anger at the chaos and at the giant bridge, which Vanbrugh wanted to be 'worthy of a Roman conqueror'.[48] The portico steps, the kitchen court, Woodstock Manor – the Duchess had a long list of complaints, and her diatribe concluded (according to Vanbrugh's letter to Lord Carlisle mentioned above) with the accusation that he had 'brought the Duke of Marlb: into this unhappy difficulty Either to leave the thing unfinishd, And by Consequence, useless to him and his Posterity; or by finishing it, to distress his Fortune, And deprive his Grandchildren of the provision he inclin'd to make for them.'

The slender thread of the relationship was snapped, and in a bitter, brilliant rejoinder, of 8 November 1716,[49] Vanbrugh wrote that the Duchess's paper was full of *Far-fetched, Labour'd Accusations, Mistaken Facts, Wrong Inferences, Groundless Jealousies and strain'd Constructions* ... You have your end Madam, for I will never trouble you more Unless the Duke of Marlborough recovers so far, to shelter me from such intolerable Treatment.' He achieved his final pitch of sarcasm by suggesting that 'your Glassmaker' – the London cabinet-maker James Moore, appointed by the Duchess as clerk of works – would 'make just such an end of the Duke's Building as her Minister Harley did of his Victories for which it was erected.' It was endorsed by the Duchess as 'a very impertinent letter of Sr Johns ...'. It was sent in the heat of the moment, and perhaps, with hindsight, caused Vanbrugh sadness, for he learned that two days later the Duke had had a second stroke.

Some work was going on, for Sir James Thornhill was at this time of rift working on the paintings in the Great Hall (**62**), but most of the master craftsmen were getting ready to leave. Wise's men were also still toiling on the bridge causeway, but he was ready to call them away home. The Comptroller, Bobart, was asked by Sarah to prepare what became known as the 'nothing done' plan[50]. With inexorable detail this formed the basis of what Sarah wrote to her counsel many years later, when the interminable Blenheim law-suits were in hand – 'This Thousands of people know, that saw it in 1716, and Some of them said it was a Chaos, and that no body but God Almighty could finish it.' The Duke was too ill to be involved in resolution of the chaos, and it was at this time that James Moore slipped into position – 'oracle', to the Duchess, or 'rogue' as many preferred it. For seven years he was in virtual charge, ignoring the keeping of accounts, that Henry Joynes had kept so meticulously, and working just enough for the owners to move in at long last. This was in 1719, 14 years after the laying of the first stone of the 'Nation's gift' to the Duke.

The Strongs were still owed money, and won their case against the Duke, who had to pay out over £12,000. Vanbrugh was jubilant[51], for an appeal had been disallowed, and his own long written 'Justification'[52] had been worth all the time he had taken on it. Its leading point was the citation of the official warrant he had been given those long years before by Lord Godolphin, appointing him Surveyor at Blenheim 'at the request and desire of the Duke of Marlborough'. There had, carefully, been no mention of the Crown, for Godolphin wanted lower rates of pay from the workmen, and thought they would accord them to the Duke better than to the State. It was all done with a lawyer's caution, but now, with the Strongs victorious, a flood of similar claims could ruin the frail Duke and his angry wife. Rising to the occasion the Duchess issued 'the Great Cause against Every Body that Had been Concern'd in that Building'.[53] It indicted some 400 persons, beginning with Vanbrugh. The Duchess was lucky in her appointed judge, Lord Macclesfield, for his own affairs were in turmoil, and he was to be impeached for bribery and corruption shortly afterwards. However his judgement included one phrase of direct concern to Vanbrugh – that he 'had noe title to demand anything out of the late Duke of Marlborough's estate for anything he did before the year 1712'.[54] Sir John was also forbidden to sue the Duke for the other two-thirds of what was due to him, the £1660 long outstanding. All the craftsmen's work was to be measured again, a long, involved process, estimated to occupy two years, and then there would be, as Vanbrugh wrote on 8 June 1721, to Lord Carlisle[55] some safety for him in not 'being pull'd to pieces by the Workmen'. But eight days later, 16 June 1722, the Duke died at Windsor Lodge, in his 73rd year.[56]

I have taken the Blenheim narrative on through the years the Duchess was in charge of the works at the house, albeit erratically, to emphasize the sharp division which came between her and Vanbrugh. Hawksmoor had been loyal to Vanbrugh and did not carry on with supervision after the latter had been dismissed. Hence, perhaps, Vanbrugh's oft-quoted remark about Hawksmoor in his letter of 26 August 1721[57] to Brigadier Watkins – 'Poor Hawksmoor, What a Barbarous Age, have his fine, ingenious Parts fallen into. What wou'd Mons[r]. Colbert in France have given for Such a Man? ...'. 'Poor Hawksmoor' it was when the Duchess bypassed him for the design of the Duke's monument, a job given to William Kent, and that of the Column of Victory, given to another Burlington disciple, Henry Herbert, the 'Architect' Earl of Pembroke. But the Duchess thought well enough of him to recommend him as Surveyor of the Fifty New Churches, and to note that had she been able to employ him, rather than Vanbrugh, 'hee would have saved the Duke of Marlborough a great summ of money'.[58]

The fact that the Strong's law-suit went against the Marlboroughs was, in view of the Duchess's well-known attitudes and her great profit from South Sea stock, lamented by few. There was nevertheless some justification for her view, expressed thus: 'If the Charge of this Building is to be fixed as a Debt upon the Duke of Marlborough, the consequence of that will be To oblige him to erect a Monument of his own Services, and to Reward himself at his own Expence; than which, it is apprehended, nothing can be more absurd.'[59] The Duke's death had however given her, in Vanbrugh's phrases, '£10,000 a Year to Spoil Blenheim, her own way, [and] £12,000 a Year to keep her Self clean, and go to Law.'[60] In addition, as he wrote a month or so later (19 July 1722)[61] to Lord Carlisle, the Duchess had £600,000 'of her own, besides what the Duke had dispos'd' which he said amounted, with jewels, plate, pictures, houses and furniture 'to a great deal above two millions'. It was no wonder therefore that, with such absolute financial power it was easy for the Duchess to demand allegiance at the risk of casting off those needing her support.

On 7 July 1725 the porter at the Woodstock Gate to Blenheim stopped Sir John Vanbrugh (his wife, and Lord Carlisle and his party) and told Lord Carlisle that 'if Sir Jno Vanbrugh or any body belonging to him was their they Must not come in'; then, as the gardener, John Hughes wrote to the Duchess[62], 'my Lord ordered the coach to go back, and told ye Porter there Should nobody come In, as belong'd to Sir Jno Vanbrugh.' Whilst some of the group – Lord Carlisle and his young people – were allowed on the next day to ride about the park, and even go into the house, Sir John had to go into the garden of Woodstock Rectory, 'and there look'd over the wall to See the water ... [and] some of the other works.' It was a sad ending to the long story about a house which remained ever close to Sir John's heart. A half-rolled plan of Blenheim appears in his left hand in the portrait of him (**125**) by Jonathan Richardson, painted in the same year of 1725.

III

Something of
the Castle Air

*As to the Outside, I thought 'twas absolutely best, to give it Something of the Castle Air,
tho' at the Same time to make it regular.*

John Vanbrugh to the Earl of Manchester
(about Kimbolton Castle), 18 July 1707.

KIMBOLTON CASTLE

It can be assumed that in 1707 Vanbrugh was occupied fully with the
building of both Castle Howard and Blenheim, but he still found time for
many other matters. The quotation at the head of this chapter shows him
writing to the Earl of Manchester, then abroad, about a medieval house
at Kimbolton, on the Cambridge borders. Vanbrugh told the Earl, alarm-
ingly, that 'the whole Garden Front has come downe', and that Lady
Manchester had asked his advice 'in carrying it up Again'.[1]

Charles Montagu, 4th Earl of Manchester (and subsequently 1st Duke)
had succeeded to his estates in 1683, but as a confirmed Whig found
himself out of favour with Charles II, and even more so with James II.
He became however an ardent supporter of William of Orange, and joined
up with him after the Torbay landing of 1688, at the head of a troop of
horse. His diplomatic career was now assured, and before the century was
out he had been ambassador extraordinary at both Venice (1697) and
Paris (1699). It was in 1707, whilst he was serving his second embassy at
Venice, that Vanbrugh wrote to him. Since his succession to the Kimbolton estates at the death of his father in France, he had been trying to
patch up the medieval home of the Mandevilles, latterly with the help of
a carpenter-joiner and builder, William Coleman. This knowledgeable
man, whom Vanbrugh was to praise in fulsome terms – 'if we had such
a Man at Blenheim he'd save us a Thousand pounds a year'[2] – had made
some plans himself.

Vanbrugh, writing fully to the Earl in his letter of 18 July 1707 tells
how, with Hawksmoor, he had gone up to Kimbolton for a discussion on
site with Coleman. His own design differed 'very much from what Coleman has drawn'. At this early stage Coleman was uncertain how to dis-

pose the rooms, and he had not been able to put the main door 'in the middle of the front'. Taken with 'many other great exceptions, both within and without' to his plan there was a need for Vanbrugh to include in his design 'some new contrivance'. This, in essence, was to suggest 'a large noble room of parade between the drawing-room and the bed-chamber' on the south side. A central door could then open from it into the garden, but, Vanbrugh demurred, he was unable to make it into a real saloon because that would have involved carrying up through into the upper storey. This would have meant destroying one of three bed-chambers, and Lady Manchester was, understandably, against doing this. However what Vanbrugh was able to provide, whilst too low for a painted ceiling, was still at least 18 feet (5.5 metres) high.[3]

Coleman, in a difficult situation for him, was cooperative, and soon discovered a 'gusto' for building the new designs. Vanbrugh told Lord Manchester that he would be 'much deceived if people do not see a manly beauty in it when it is up'. This 'manly beauty' was to come from giving the elevations 'Something of the Castle Air' (**80**) and to do this through the 'figure and proportions', rather than any 'delicacy of the ornaments'. He would be able to use the old stone, and thus blend in the new facades with the rest. Apart from a desire to obey Alberti's edict on conformity, his solutions were entirely in accord with what needed to be done to give the castle air to a medieval building. He could also see that everything was given a symmetrical appearance, and this was emphasized by binding the fronts together with square (rusticated) pilasters. There are several other examples of this, in Vanbrugh's work, such as, his own house at Whitehall (**3**), the north front at Castle Howard (**11**), the Blenheim facades (**11**) or, in a further variation (ringed columns in groups of three), at Seaton Delaval. The saloon projection was now put in hand, and Vanbrugh was pleased with its appearance as it rose: it 'looks mighty pleasantly Up the Middle of the Garden and Canall'.[4] He did however predict that when Lord Manchester was at home again, he would be tempted to take down and rebuild all the outside walls round the castle. Three more letters from Vanbrugh to his patron survive, all written between May and August 1708, and in the last of them (17 August), Vanbrugh notes his pleasure that Lord Manchester is 'order'd home'. He assured him the shell of the building would be complete, and that the apartments within would be worthy of the 'good furniture you have provided for it'.

The Earl, whilst in Venice, had tried to enlist the Republic's support of the Grand Alliance against Louis XIV – a mission which failed. He had time however to pick out painters to work for him at Kimbolton. From Luca Carlevarijs he first commissioned a canvas (now in the Birmingham Art Gallery) showing his landing at the Piazzetta. Pellegrini, and Marco

Ricci were persuaded to come to England with the Earl when he returned in the winter of 1708. Vanbrugh had told him firmly, however, that 'the New Room at Kimbolton can't be ready for him [Pellegrini] this winter. So I suppose you'll Set him Upon the Hall'.[5] This didn't happen, but for the time being there was work for the painters at Castle Howard (**33**); Vanbrugh too was over-busy at Blenheim and with the Opera. As well as painters the Earl had sought out opera singers, and it was also he who induced Handel to come to England.

With Lord Manchester back in England Vanbrugh exerted more pressure on him to have the whole castle refaced in stone. Coleman and his men were soon hard at this on the east and west fronts. Inside, the south saloon and the other rooms had still not been given their floorboards by 1710; but by the end of that year the staircase was ready for painting by Pellegrini. With so much of his work at Castle Howard destroyed in the 1940 fire the paintings at Kimbolton (chapel and staircase) are now his most important surviving achievement in England[6]: they are statements, in oil on plaster, of colourful exuberance. That on the staircase shows the triumphal procession of a Roman emperor, attended by musicians in a feigned balcony, and with joyous *putti* holding a medallion of Lord Manchester far above on the ceiling. In the 1710 accounts there are also two entries for drawing paper, and postage for 'draughts sent from London' by Nicholas Hawksmoor. He was acting, as he was to do so often, as the capable assistant in day-to-day matters. It did not prove possible to do everything Vanbrugh wanted, and on the east front the Doric portico was created finally, in 1719, by the Florentine architect Alessandro Galilei.

CHARGATE

We have seen earlier that in 1700-1 Vanbrugh had been allowed to build his small house in the ruins of Whitehall Palace (**3**), which, in 1703 drew forward Swift's first versified comments, ending:

> ... At length they in the rubbish spy
> A thing resembling a Goose-Pye.

Swift's versifying did not please Vanbrugh, and Swift later told Stella (in 1710) that Vanbrugh had a long quarrel with him about the two sets of verses – the second written in 1708. According to Swift, 'we were very civil and cold', and Vanbrugh was teased with them, by of all persons, the Duchess of Marlborough.[7] They may have led him to consider building on a grander scale for himself on many an occasion, but another small box, Chargate, at Esher, was what he actually planned. He built it in about 1709 in the parish next to where his mother was living, albeit for a short time as she died in August 1711. It was far enough from the court and from the prying eyes of satirical poets to allow him to create at will all the embattled facades he wished, with a powerful broken-pedimented centrepiece (**83–84**), and arched and vaulted corridors within. It has been called 'a castle in a nursery, a romantic toy',[8] but like all castles which expressed the distilled essence of rivalry to a marauding monarch, it too vanished quickly. Vanbrugh's finances were in a great muddle over the failure of the Opera House and his salary at Blenheim was always being delayed: the death of his mother had meant the settlement of funeral expenses, and as one of his few assets was Chargate it had to be sold. The buyer, the Earl of Clare (afterwards the Duke of Newcastle), was to become one of Vanbrugh's closest friends over the next few years. With succession to the estates of his uncle secure even if they were heavily mortgaged, the Earl could afford to use Vanbrugh to enlarge Chargate, which he then renamed, after his title, as 'Claremont'.

It is not relevant in a short study of Vanbrugh to pursue too closely all that was done to enlarge Claremont, especially as it no longer survives. The small house was swallowed up in the larger one, but was demolished in 1763, to be replaced by a new house (1771–4) designed by 'Capability' Brown and Henry Holland.[9] Only the Belvedere Tower (**86**) and the White Cottage were allowed to survive. The brick-built Belvedere, with its four towers, allowed visitors to take in what Campbell in *Vitruvius Britannicus* (III, 77) had called 'a most prodigious fine Prospect of the Thames and the adjacent villas'. The White Cottage or 'Mr Greening's House' is shown only in Rocque's drawing, dated 1738.[10] What these small buildings demonstrate, as with the many Vanbrugh drawings for small houses (**94–96**), is that the architect was adept at blending 'something of the medieval picturesqueness with the ordered dignity of classic architecture', and giving to them all a conformity that accorded with Renaissance thought.

KING'S WESTON

Like three other Vanbrugh houses (Eastbury, Seaton Delaval and Grimsthorpe), King's Weston was begun for one generation and finished for the next. About 1710–11, Edward Southwell asked Vanbrugh to design a house on earlier foundations, on property set on rising ground above the Bristol Channel. He had inherited in 1702 at the death of his father, Sir Robert Southwell, and like him became Secretary of State for Ireland. He was also appointed as Clerk to the Privy Council[12], and was 39 years old at the start of building.

King's Weston is a small house with strong elevations and chimney arcading (**87, 89**). We know that the walls were up by 1713, for on 23 October 1713 Vanbrugh wrote whilst at Castle Howard to Edward Southwell[13] that he was 'pleased with the house being quite covered in so good season', and that it would therefore dry out much quicker than normal.

In order that the all-important silhouette should match that in the architect's imagination, he would arrange (as at Blenheim) to proceed with the
chimneys only when: 'I was with you on the spot, to make tryall of the
heights etc, with boards.' Southwell, anxious to be ahead, had already
had the scaffolding cleared: he would have to wait to see if Vanbrugh's
belief was correct that King's Weston would have the same comforts as
Lord Carlisle had at Castle Howard ('every room in the house is like an
oven').

The master-mason employed at King's Weston was George Townesend
of Bristol, a son of John Townesend of Oxford, who had worked for Vanbrugh at Blenheim. There is in existence a 'Book of Designs'[14] made up
by an anonymous compiler for Southwell, in which there is a drawing
signed in 1717 by Townesend. Vanbrugh planned the principal elevation
to face south (**87**). There is the usual rhythmic display of square cut
Corinthian pilasters on the engaged portico, in the pattern 2.1.1.2., surmounted by a dominant pediment which contains a lunette window. The
arcaded chimneystacks form a three-sided feature on the roof, above the
centre of each facade.

Inside the house the staircase (**88**) was the least altered feature in the
remodelling undertaken in 1763–8 by Robert Mylne.[15] A drawing survives
in the King's Weston album for the parquetry 'of the half paces of the
great staircase' dated 1719–20. The walls surrounding it are arcaded, with
niches painted in grisaille to depict urns and statues. This was a decorative
device favoured by both Vanbrugh and Hawksmoor. The hall at Grimsthorpe (**118, 120**) has similar paintings, but of English Kings, and there
are lavish paintings by Thornhill on the staircase at Easton Neston.[16] A
variation was provided at Seaton Delaval (**111**) by the use of stucco
statues within niches, possibly by Giovanni Bagutti, who had worked for
Vanbrugh at Castle Howard.

In February 1717–18 Vanbrugh had projected a forecourt to the house,
to be surrounded by a low wall having a ha-ha outside and below it. The
south entrance was to have been approached through a massive gateway,
similar to that surviving at Eastbury (**79**). The drawing[17] shows an archway, surmounted by a pyramid, not dissimilar to the Pyramid Gate at
Castle Howard (**31**), and rising overall to some 40 feet (12 metres). However, this interesting feature was not built – but the Weston album does
contain several drawings for Vanbrughian doorways (one for the east
garden door, dated 26 March 1722) and chimneypieces, as well as many
projects for stables and garden buildings at King's Weston. They are
characterized by machicolated towers, arched windows, and pedimented
gables; that for a projected ale-house (June 1718) has a small
pyramidal-topped circular tower, foreshadowing what Vanbrugh was to
build at his own castle at Greenwich (**99–100**).

THE GREENWICH ESTATE

Apart from his house Chargate, his official one in Whitehall, and short stays at Woodstock and at his wife's Yorkshire home, Heslington, Vanbrugh's main residence from the time of his marriage in 1719 was at Greenwich. He had a long connection with the area, through the appointment in 1695 of his brother William as Secretary to the Hospital Committee. He had also been knighted there in 1714 by George I, and was appointed, two years later, to succeed Wren as the Hospital Surveyor. It was therefore very appropriate to take a lease in 1718 on a piece of high ground at the south-east corner of Greenwich Park. On it he built not only a contrived medley of walls, towers and battlements as a house, but something which announced to all his medieval, castle-like interests. As he may also have been at Kimbolton, Vanbrugh was probably as concerned with 'advocating conformity and unity of style' – or 'the old Renaissance concept of *conformità*, as with 'a desire for the revival of medievalism'.[18] There was also space for three more buildings – Vanbrugh House (or 'Mince-Pie House') to be occupied by his brother Charles, The Nunnery (for Philip Vanbrugh), and the two White Towers, which Vanbrugh built for his sons, Charles and John (**2**), but which he bequeathed to his sisters, Robina and Victoria.[19]

It has been suggested that 'The Nunnery' was so titled because Philip Vanbrugh was a widower, and perhaps looked after by his unmarried sisters. Whatever the exact arrangement, the Vanbrughs were within easy calling distance of each other. At the Maze Hill end of the site, and at a distance of about half a mile from his relatives, was Greenwich Castle itself (**99-100**). When Vanbrugh built it in 1717 he gave it a symmetrical plan, with a round staircase tower at the centre, two towers on the south corners, and a projecting bow window on the north side. The expectation of children after his marriage in 1719 – Charles was born in October 1720, and John in January 1721/2 (**2**) – caused him to enlarge the castle, and in doing so 'he created a building which is remarkable – and at its date without precedent – for its new found asymmetry.'[20]

Throughout the 25 years or so in which Vanbrugh was concerned with architecture he continued to be influenced by the architecture of castles. The assemblages of towers, outworks, and battlements, seemingly so suitable as a stage set, were present in his early work – for example at Kimbolton in 1708 – and act as an important exemplar to the picturesque buildings which were erected later in the eighteenth century. It was their gaunt silhouette which appealed to the visual sense of Sir Joshua Reynolds, who, in his *13th Discourse* (1786) noted that it was towers and battlements that were so often selected by poet and painter to make 'a part of the composition of their landscape'. Vanbrugh was both poet and architect, continued Reynolds, and in his buildings 'there is a greater display of imagination, than we shall perhaps find in any other.'[21] The Castle is now the only survival on the Greenwich estate, but before the demolition of the other houses at the turn of this century surveys were made and photographs taken.[22]

DIVERS COMMISSIONS

Any architect as near the centre of official building activity as Vanbrugh inevitably took on work for friends and acquaintances, beyond what he supervised for the Board of Works. In particular the Duke of Newcastle asked for his help at his London house, and at Nottingham Castle, and there were amendments to interiors for Lord Bindon at Audley End (**82**), Sir Robert Walpole, and for George, Prince of Wales. The Duke of Newcastle had also acquired two houses in Lincoln's Inn Fields which needed rebuilding. Vanbrugh wrote to the Duke on February 5, 1714-15[23] apprising him that the workmen there had been busy as 'a Swarm of Bees', and that it would be ready shortly if the upholsterer did not cause delays. The rooms had been given new chimneypieces, seemingly of Derbyshire marble, and provided by John Thorp of Bakewell. He had agreed in 1717 with Sir Charles Hotham (for whom Colen Campbell was working) to make two marble chimneypieces 'equal in size and all other respects' to two 'great chimney pieces' which he mentioned he had sold to the Duke of Newcastle. Vanbrugh had therefore kept in touch with Thorp, who had done a great deal of work on the floors and chimneypieces at Castle Howard in 1711-12.[24]

The house in Lincoln's Inn Fields was to be given decorative paintings, seemingly by John Vanderbank (1694-1739), son of the tapestry weaver to the Great Wardrobe. Vanbrugh told the Duke that 'the Middle room in the Great Appartment above Stairs, will be ready before Mr Vanderbank, but not by the end of this month ...'. Vanderbank had presumably come to Vanbrugh's notice as an original member of Sir Godfrey Kneller's academy. This also included as members Laguerre, Pellegrini, and Thornhill, all of whom worked in Vanbrugh houses, and Kneller had painted Sir John's portrait for the Kit-Cat Club series he had done of all the members to be presented to the club secretary, Jacob Tonson.

In the work he did for Sir Robert Walpole Vanbrugh knew he was dealing with not only the Prime Minister but an astute financier, who was later to make a further fortune from prudent speculation in South Sea stock. Writing on 17 October 1715[25] about Walpole House in Chelsea Vanbrugh told Sir Robert that whilst he had made 'an estimate of your fabrick, which comes to £270' he had allowed for doing some things in a better manner 'than perhaps you will think necessary'. It could be done for £200, but to provide further satisfaction, he intended to give the facts to Sir Robert's clerk of works, allow him to make his own calculation, and then give 'each particular article to the respective workmen; and they shall make their estimation too'. It was meant to please, and the letter concluded with the hope that 'you shall know the bottom of it, at last; or the Devil shall be in it'. Walpole House was a useful London base for a busy politician. However it can no longer be seen for after being converted into part of Chelsea Hospital in 1809, it was demolished in 1941.[26]

In 1716, Vanbrugh was embroiled in troubles beyond mere building with Sarah, Duchess of Marlborough, through having started to act, at her request, as match maker between the Duke of Newcastle and Sarah's grand-daughter. He was also busy with amending Claremont, assuring the Duke, 'I am Swearing as much as is necessary to get it cover'd', and that Newcastle House in Lincoln's Inn Fields 'will soon be ready'.[27] It was vital for many personal causes that Vanbrugh remained within the Duke's patronage, and he hurried the Smallwells and the Hopsons,[28] accomplished joiners, to the various houses Newcastle owned. What evolved at Claremont was unusual in both plan and appearance, caused by a considerable scheme of addition and enlargement. Its 'exaggerated receding forecourt and successive towers' were at least 'very characteristic of Vanbrugh',[29] and are shown both in an engraving by J. Rocque of 1738, and in a drawing attributed to J. F. Rigaud, c 1750.[30]

In 1674 William Cavendish, 1st Duke of Newcastle (1st creation) had bought the site of the medieval castle at Nottingham, and built himself a palace on it, completed in 1679. It gives a first appearance 'that is, in its general shape, with the top balustrade, as if it stood in North Italy or Prague'.[31] The Castle passed ultimately into the hands of John Holles, who married Margaret Cavendish, co-heiress of the Duke of Newcastle, a title to which he had succeeded in 1694. His nephew, Thomas Pelham-Holles, Vanbrugh's friend, took the name of Holles when succeeding his uncle, and was created anew as Duke of Newcastle in 1715. It was natural that after using Vanbrugh to remodel Claremont the new Duke should retain him to do the same at Nottingham Castle. Vanbrugh first visited the Castle in 1718, and he wrote to the Duke on 17 December that it was on as 'horrible a day, as Storms, hail, Snow and the Divil can make it'.[32] He pronounced that there was space for stables and outbuildings, and an agreeable Castle garden 'of near three Acres of ground', actually within the Castle Walls. He also cautioned about too much haste in building during the winter months and advised that only painting, glazing and whitewashing go on 'and leave the rest till I can attend you here in April or May . . .'.

What Vanbrugh did at Nottingham was, alas, destroyed in the fire of 1831, but as with all his houses he was concerned about its appearance. He looked at what the Duke of Rutland was doing at Belvoir Castle 'where for want of being rightly understood, the whole grace' of the outworks 'is lost', and advised the Duke of Newcastle that a better effect could be achieved at Nottingham. The arrangement suggested in the surviving letters was for Vanbrugh to meet the Duke at the Castle in December 1718, but on Christmas Day he was isolated at a snow-bound Castle Howard. It was an auspicious day on which to write his oft-quoted remark: 'In short, tis so bloody Cold, I have almost a mind to Marry to keep myself warm . . .'.[33] Nottingham Castle was to be the Duke's northern seat, and Vanbrugh, still snowed in at Castle Howard, lamented that the Duke had been to Nottingham, thus seeing it at its winter worst. He wrote for instructions of what the Duke felt needed to be done. He was relieved to find in a further quick interchange of letters that the Duke had not been discouraged 'from thinking it practicable to live upon a Precipice a hundred ft. high'.[34] We hear no more in letters to the Duke about Nottingham Castle, but much of Claremont, of eating the Duke's venison, of wishing to be drunk upon his birthday, but railing still at the upheaval in the Board of Works following the episodes over William Benson's appointment. Only his marriage in 1719 enlivened a difficult period, but as he wrote to Newcastle on 11 August, 'I am not one of those, who drop their Spirits on every Rebuff.'

The last architectural design Vanbrugh made in 1723[35] for the Duke of Newcastle was to design him a pew in Esher Church (**85**), although a year later he was still bothering about garden seats for the waterside at Claremont. The design for the pew was copied out fair by Vanbrugh's draughtsman, Arthur (his surname is not known). Subsequently divided, to facilitate use by the Duke's brother, it still presents a grand temple front, with many allusions to classical Italy. It was complete by 1725,[36] within a year of the architect's death and when he was writing to Tonson (12 August) that 'you will perhaps think me a little chang'd (and not for the better)'. He had just paid a visit to Blenheim, where he had been denied access by the Duchess.

EASTBURY PARK

Of this great Dorset house near Blandford, the largest Vanbrugh designed after Castle Howard and Blenheim, only part of the kitchen court, and a great arch survive (**78–79**). Also its builder, George Dodington, a cousin of Viscount Cobham of Stowe, did not survive to see the house complete: nor did his architect. After Dodington's death in 1720 his son George Bubb Dodington, Baron Melcombe, 'the apotheosis of pompous unction and back stairs politics'[37] delayed restarting the works at the house until 1724. Eastbury was completed by Roger Morris in 1733–8, 'by which time it had served as the centre for a group of friends including Vanbrugh,

Thornhill, Christopher Pitt, Edward Young, and James Thomson.'[38] The latter put a description of Eastbury and its landscape, laid out by Charles Bridgeman, into the Autumn section of *The Seasons* (1730).

About 1709 George Dodington bought a farm on the edge of Cranborne Chase but before he was through it had expanded, through Vanbrugh's fertile imagination, to a 'palace' of five courts, with a total length of over 570 feet (175 metres). The designs for the house are in several stages, with those marked for a 'Person of Quality in Dorsetshire' appearing in the second volume (1717) of Campbell's *Vitruvius Britannicus* (**70–72**). It is stated in a poem of Christopher Pitt's, written in 1722, that wooden models were prepared in order to visualize the intended whole, and two paintings still survive, to show its final extent (**76–77**).

One of the earliest sketches, almost certainly in Vanbrugh's hand (**68**), 'was made between 1709 and 1716, [and] probably not earlier than 1713.' It is a version of that for the entrance front (**70**) published by Campbell, but with two Venetian openings in place of the Corinthian portico. The distinctive arcaded chimneystacks have been introduced, but the overall scale is still restrained. Two other drawings, more carefully ruled in ink and tinted, were then submitted. That of the Garden Front is illustrated here (**69**); its companion, for the 'Fore Front'[39], shows, by the scale, that the width had been increased marginally. The bow on the garden front was flanked by an extra Corinthian column, and subsequent drawings show the house extended by pavilions,[40] with the bow rising to the full height of the garden front. This was engraved as one of the 'New Designs' for Campbell's second volume in 1717.

The side elevation (**72**) was also improved significantly with Venetian windows, and coupled columns. These features, part of the earlier entrance front (**68**) were moved from there in order to incorporate the portico. Something of this growth can be seen by reference to the final plan (**71**) published in 1725, which shows the kitchen court (marked 'M') to the east, instead of the west, as usual in a Vanbrugh scheme.[41] The transition from designs for a small house to those for a medium and then a larger one may not have been satisfactory to the owner, or to his architect. It is however known that George Bubb Dodington lost money in the South Sea financial trouble, in 1720–1, and this had altered his intent, and the progress of the building.[42] Nevertheless the courts in a characteristic touch of 'theatre' were given the great gateways, 'Roman, Baroque and Medieval all at once' in Tipping and Hussey's phrase. One of them survives (**79**), Cyclopean, and with two pine trees growing from its top.

The later designs for the house being so altered in scale meant that, either by accident or intention, the men (including, perhaps, John Chapman as mason) started on the wings of the forecourt, and the base courts to the sides. It was a reversal of what Vanbrugh had done at Castle Howard, or at Blenheim. Something of the original disposition of this main elevation can be seen in a painting at Eastbury (**76**). It shows the great length of the forecourt arcades, but as only nine arches of the 21 originals now survive on the north side (**78**) we do not know for certain whether the wings were ever fully built. The painting could have been based on Campbell's plan, or the wings shortened when the main house was demolished. However the latter seems correct for Whistler has noted that the outline of the whole mansion, including extended forecourts, has been detected by the owners in a dry summer.[43]

In working out differences between the 'New Designs' and the final ones, it is apparent that Vanbrugh reduced the width of the main block by turning the entrance hall round, and then put towers out at the four corners, to mask the consequent narrowing effect.

A further variant in design even shows an unusual round hall with eight columns supporting a cupola,[44] a version perhaps of that intended originally for Blenheim. The final entrance front (**74**), published in the third volume of *Vitruvius Britannicus* (1725), shows the arcaded chimneys containing windows, which were intended to light the internal staircase. The amendments persisted – this feature was not carried out, and the portico *in antis*, with its ringed columns, was even given a pediment (perhaps by Roger Morris) after Vanbrugh's death. The final plan (**71**) shows two octagons on the garden front (**77**) which were intended to contain a chapel (marked 'H') and an 'Eating room' ('I'). Their painted decoration was entrusted to Sir James Thornhill, and it has been assumed that the Chapel was given an 'Ascension' on its ceiling, with 'Roses & Mouldings to be heightened with gold'. The eating room, probably, had the 'Venus, Ceres and Bacchus' depicted in a Thornhill sketch, inscribed: 'Historys proper for a dining Room, Or to ye Pavilion of a seat in Hunting Country'.[45] At some point between 1733, the date of a sketch by Morris[46], and about 1760, the date of the two paintings, the pyramid roofs to the two octagon rooms were removed. In 1775 the greater part of the house was demolished with gunpowder.

We have referred to Vanbrugh's great interest in gardens, strengthened through his friendship with Joseph Addison, and his own theatrical and literary knowledge. Whilst much of what was done to the surrounding demesnes to his houses was under the skilled control of Charles Bridgeman (or at Blenheim of both Henry Wise and Bridgeman), there is no doubt that the architect watched over the various schemes with an informed concern. At Eastbury, we know from a plan of the gardens attributed to Bridgeman, and from that in Colen Campbell's book (III, 1725, pl. 15) that the parterres and water were set in a great formal pattern around the house, and perhaps for once, in a more symmetrical mode than Vanbrugh preferred. The radiating walks however did lead to views over shaped mounts and banks, and to a many-levelled amphitheatre, the ghostly outlines of which can still be seen. The garden walls were of course pierced by doorways, but these were as nothing to the surviving entrance gateway to the park, piled high with square-cut banded piers, and ball finials.[47] There was, within sight of the house, a temple, and a bagnio (or water pavilion) surrounded by a 'vast Collection of foreign trees of various Kinds'.[48] The bagnio had (**75**) a rusticated basement, niches between Ionic columns, and a pediment proudly bearing a coat-of-arms, but nothing of it now remains. The Temple itself has also gone: as engraved for Campbell, it was a vast pedimented structure, set off by soaring Corinthian columns, and almost as high as the south front of Seaton Delaval, or the pediment of James Gibbs's St Martin-in-the-Fields.[49] Its platform, like so much in this intriguing garden – 'one of the finest collaborations in English design'[50] – is all there now is to show where it stood. Only imagination can again rear it up, or stretch out the long, deep-cut facades of Eastbury itself, born of a mind of rare originality. Whilst this had been set to work by 'a Person of Quality in Dorsetshire', Vanbrugh needed little urging to bring touches of theatrical ingenuity to any garden building, or even to any of the greater houses.

On 3 September 1719 the princely James Brydges, 1st Duke of Chandos, wrote to Robert Benson, Lord Bingley '[that if] my little building ... shou'd be such an one as is displeasing to your Lordship I shall pull it down with more satisfaction than I carry it up....' It was the age of sacrifice to the dictates of the great Goddess of Taste. What James Brydges was ready to do at Cannons, where Vanbrugh often dined at the Officers' table, Sir Richard Temple (created Viscount Cobham in 1714) was ready to do almost in reverse at Stowe: he carried up with more satisfaction than at pulling down. For his gardens 'he engaged the best men he could find to plan them. Charles Bridgeman, just then emerging as heir apparent to Henry Wise, was commissioned for the lay-out, and Sir John Vanbrugh, already at the head of his profession, was asked to design the buildings to embellish it.'[51] In fact on July 1, 1719 Vanbrugh wrote to Jacob Tonson a letter in which he also told him of his marriage:[52]

> I lately went to make my Ld. Cobham a Visit at Stowe, where he is very well, and in very good humour: and much entertain'd with (besides his wife) the Improvements of his House and Gardens, in which he spends all he has to spare....

The two, Vanbrugh and Bridgeman, had already worked at Eastbury for Lord Cobham's cousin, George Dodington. Sir Richard, as he then was, had been a distinguished compatriot of the Duke of Marlborough in the wars against Louis XIV, and was also, like Vanbrugh, a member of the convivial Kit-Cat Club. Sir Richard must often have turned his mind, with that of the Duke of Marlborough, to building matters, then in charge of the erstwhile soldier, Vanbrugh. The inheritance of a late seventeenth-century house from his father, Sir Richard Temple (d. 1697) gave the younger Sir Richard the chance to alter the formal gardens, to plans which, whilst geometrical, abandoned symmetry. 'Aerial' views, both in bird's-eye view engravings and photographs, are available to demonstrate this.[53] Bridgeman seems to have started work at Stowe in 1714 – at least there is a payment to 'Mr bridgemans man' in that year. It may have been 1716 before Vanbrugh joined him, on his banishment from Blenheim.[54]

On the north side of the house Vanbrugh raised the four corners as towers, with the dormers being hidden behind a balustrade. At this time, in the early 1720s, the north portico (**101–102**) was added. It has been attributed at various times to William Kent, and to Giacomo Leoni (it is similar to that by Leoni at Lyme Hall, Cheshire), but its use of double columns, square with round, have tilted the attribution back in recent years as a Vanbrugh achievement. Interestingly, with his keen knowledge of the theories of Alberti, Vanbrugh had subscribed in advance in 1721 for Leoni's translation, published finally in 1726 (**5**). The north front at Stowe remained as Vanbrugh had formed it for some 40 years, but amendments, such as an attic between the towers, a row of urns, and the graceful Neo-Classical colonnades, were added by Earl Temple in the early 1770s.[55]

The gardens at Stowe are filled with many important temples, buildings and obelisks designed by Vanbrugh, Gibbs and Kent, although there have of course been subsequent embellishments and amendments. It is necessary to note the buildings by Vanbrugh which survive: the two Lake Pavilions (on the south-east shore of the Octagon Lake, near to the Cascade) which were rebuilt in 1764. North-west of the Cascade is the Rotunda, built to Vanbrugh's design in 1721, but again altered, by Borra, in 1752. It stands at a cross-point of the old gardens, 'with radiating lines in several directions' and locks 'together the whole design'. The dome was once of a more rounded shape, on Roman Ionic columns, with a gilt statue of Venus within, as shown in Rigaud's view (**103**). The shafts of the columns, 'the inspiration and general form', are still however Vanbrugh's: he had given 'another version of the humble English mount with seat and rails' by transmuting it 'into garden architecture'.[56]

In his bird's-eye view engraving of Stowe[57] Charles Bridgeman depicted seven garden features 'by Vanbrugh, or attributable to him: – Nelson's Seat, the two Lake Pavilions, the Brick Temple (or Temple of Bacchus), the Guglio Fountain, Coucher's Obelisk, and the Rotunda. In addition the Temple of Sleep, the Cold Bath, and the Pyramid were Vanbrugh's, though none is indicated.'[58] There is also some reason for attributing King

George's Column and the Witch's House to him. It all added up to a considerable phase of garden activity and building. Vanbrugh, at Stowe on several occasions, wrote on 12 August 1725, to Tonson about one visit.[59] 'The Company were so well pleas'd at Stowe, that they stay'd four days, My Lord Carlisle then went on to Castle Howard, and we Stay'd at Stowe a Fortnight, a Place now, so Agreeable, that I had much ado to leave it at all.' Peering over a wall at one's creation was a sad substitute for pacing the gravelled works to the correct viewing-point atop the mount, and Vanbrugh must have found the two patrons and settings a sharp contrast. In the company of Lord Cobham, and of Lord Carlisle, he was able to inform Tonson that 'if you come to Towne' we shall meet 'Not as a Club, but old Friends that have been of a Club, and the best Club, that ever met.' On the strength of knowing Club members commissions were awarded, preferments obtained, and perhaps even a chuckle raised with them, at Vanbrugh's words: 'I have given my everlasting Friend the Dutchess of Marlb: Great trouble lately ...'.[60] There were many who would applaud, who were timid at the thought of saying so themselves.

SEATON DELAVAL

It is easy, if one has space for long description, to be effusive about Seaton Delaval, the Vanbrugh ruin – the interior of the centre block was badly damaged by fire in 1822 – on the Northumbrian coast. Tipping and Hussey were able to do so in 1927: 'the wheels crunch frost-bound gravel ... and you turn into the great court before this winter palace. Hollow eyes watch you from blind windows high in gigantic walls, and the wind howls among the balustraded battlements.' The stuff of Gothick novels, and, alas, not much to our purpose here, although the great court before the north front is impressive enough, a triumph of what could even be called 'Picturesque', but blended together with a Baroque richness.

In February 1717 Admiral George Delaval, a man of action, and owner already of much property, acquired Seaton from Sir John, the last of the elder line of Delavals. He was then anxious to see if he could persuade Vanbrugh 'to give me a plan of a house, or to alter the old one, which he is most excellent at ...'.[61] There might well have been a stifled moan from Sir John at this, but as it transpired he was able to build Seaton Delaval, untrammelled, as on other occasions, by the confines of any previous walls or foundations.

A few fragmentary documentary references to the house have come to light in recent years, but for the moment the first letter we have from Vanbrugh about Seaton Delaval is the frequently quoted one to Brigadier Watkins of 26 August 1721,[62] where he also refers to 'Several Gentlemen in the(se) Parts of the World, that are possess'd w(ith) the Spirit of

Building ...'. Writing of Seaton Delaval he noted: 'I have been near three weeks, finding a vast deal to do, both at Delavals and Lumley Castle.... The Admiral is very Gallant in his operations, not being dispos'd to starve the Design at all. So that he is like to have, a very fine Dwelling for himself, now, and his Nephew &c hereafter.' What Vanbrugh then arranged, at York, was that his clerk of works at Seaton would be the talented William Etty (*d.* 1734), scion of a distinguished family of York mason-joiners. It is however in a letter[63] from Sir William Robinson to his son Metcalfe, of 5 June 1721 that we learn that: 'Etty ... is gone to Admirall De Lavalls to lay ye foundation of his house, and will return next week ...'. Etty was working for Sir William at his Yorkshire house of Baldersby, then building to Colen Campbell's designs.[64]

The mannered facades of Seaton Delaval (**106–108**) rely on the use of emphatic recessions, heavy-ringed double columns on each side of the front door, angled towers and the stretching forward arms of the stable and kitchen wings, at east and west respectively, enclosing the grassy forecourt. Within the south front pediment Vanbrugh put his favourite lunette window, and as at King's Weston (**87**) this may have been based on noting the (less dominantly) positioned example at Palladio's Villa Barbaro at Maser. Dr Lang has discussed Vanbrugh's view of Palladio as being 'the country house builder *par excellence*, from whom one could borrow not only plans and motifs but above all solutions of problems.'[65] She also drew attention to the interior division of the Villa Pogliano as being 'nearly identical with that of Seaton Delaval', with the Villa Zero at Cessalto, and the Villa di Angarano contributing certain other details. We know that Vanbrugh had a French edition of Palladio, with plans – presumably the Martin of 1650 – that he had subscribed to Leoni's edition in English, Italian and French of 1715,[66] and that his Temple at Castle Howard was also (soon) to be based on Palladio's most famous villa, 'La Rotunda' (or the Villa Almerico), built for Paolo Almerico, south-east of Vicenza. It was a subtle borrowing from the engraved forms of pediments, windows and columns, which seemed to lose little in being set up in three dimensions on a stark windswept site such as Seaton Delaval, rather than a sunnier hilltop in the Veneto.

In the setting-up and supervision of Seaton Delaval Vanbrugh relied on William Etty, who is mentioned in some papers[67] displayed in the house. One bears architectural directions and a rough sketch for the semi-circular window above the main north entrance (**106**) but it is headed 'George Cansfield, August ye 16, 1722'. Additionally there are building accounts – one for six months ending 2 April 1721, a similar account ending 6 April 1724, and 'An Account of Mr Etty's Days at Seaton Delaval', 1723–4, with notes of the quantity of ale he drank and of the oats eaten by his horse. There are two letters from James Mewburn;

the first, of 12 October 1719 refers to quarrying of stone and treeplanting, and the second, undated, is to an unidentified correspondent about the progress on the building and the panelling of the North East Room. There is also a small group of Delaval papers elsewhere[68] which supplement those at the house; one mentions a design by Vanbrugh for the East Staircase.

In the forecourt 15 steps rise to the North Entrance door which opens into the Hall. The interior of this centre block now looks a little like a scene in one of Piranesi's *Carceri* engravings, for the 1822 fire destroyed its ceiling, and a great void rises through the upper storey to the high roof. A robust gallery (**111**) supported on carved console brackets crosses from east to west, as at Castle Howard (**63**) and Blenheim. The niches in the upper half of the walls are filled, not with grisaille paintings as at King's Weston (**127**) and Grimsthorpe (**120**), but with stucco statues representing the liberal arts. These are attributed to Giovanni Bagutti, the stuccoist from Rovio, near Lugano, whose first work in England (1709–12) was for Vanbrugh at Castle Howard. The statues were calcined to near-destruction in the fire, which exposed something of their terracotta and metal armature cores, and showed the hessian drapery, formerly swathed across the figure and set in position by being dipped in gypsum.

Beyond the Hall is the gutted Saloon or Gallery – divided into three sections by semi-screens of square Corinthian columns, four to each – and having, originally, a painted ceiling. Through the Saloon access was also gained to the south front, with its magnificent fluted Ionic columns, rearing pediment, and view of the two staircase towers. There are some similarities here to the (vanished) garden front at Eastbury, but this can now only be seen in a surviving painting (**77**).

The house archives include 'A note of the whole expenses of building Seaton Delaval Hall up to 3 April 1725' amounting to £6262.1.3½.[69] There is a certain subtle irony that with such a fine stable block, of true Vanbrughian grandeur with an exciting Baroque interior (**109**), Admiral Delaval met his death by falling from his horse, which he had mounted one afternoon for a tour of his then still incomplete house. His nephew Francis, succeeded him, and as the new heir to the continuing income from coal and the little port of Seaton Sluice (which held back the waters until the tide was out) carried it all to completion,[70] three years after Vanbrugh's death. In point of 'movement, novelty and ingenuity' it has not been bettered.

LUMLEY CASTLE

Something of the 'Castle Air', even if that was concerned in part with suggesting Renaissance conformity, could be said to pervade Lumley Castle, Durham, which Vanbrugh added to in 1722. He first referred to the Castle in his important letter of 26 August 1721 to Brigadier Watkins:

'Lumley Castle is a Noble thing; and well deserves the Favours Lord Lumley designs to bestow upon it; In order to which, I stay'd there near a Week, to form a General Design for the whole ...'[71] He continued in words worthy of Sir Henry Wotton or Sir Balthazar Gerbier that he intended to alter the house for 'State, Beauty and Convenience', and to do it for a sum which would never 'ly very heavy upon the Family'. Here, at last was a great castle, crenellated in the reign of Richard II, and fully worthy of Vanbrugh's attention. At Richard Lumley's death in 1721 (he had been created Earl of Scarbrough by William III) the succession passed to his son, another Richard, born in 1688, the year of William III's accession. As Lord Lumley he had sat in the House of Lords during his father's lifetime, but as a Lord of the Bedchamber, and Master of the House to the Prince of Wales (later George II) he would know of Vanbrugh and his circle of influential friends. In his father's last year of life, he asked Vanbrugh to look over the Castle, with a view to amending it to his own needs.

The exterior changes were few – Vanbrugh pierced the west front (**105**) with sashed windows, and some windows of a circular shape. He provided graceful new steps, and terraces, but within there were few amendments to the medieval layout. It was done carefully and the new Baroque garb was not allowed to disturb the Elizabethan chimneypiece in the Hall or the Richard II windows to the Inner Court. Thus it was that Lumley was given a capable adjustment of old forms to new requirements, but the dramatic outline was still that of Ralph Lumley's fourteenth-century Castle. Alas, Lord Scarbrough enjoyed it all for only 15 years or so. He committed suicide in 1740 on the eve of his marriage to the Duchess of Manchester, grand-daughter of the 1st Duke of Marlborough.

GRIMSTHORPE CASTLE

Grimsthorpe Castle was the last house to be designed by Sir John Vanbrugh, but it is a very worthy representative of his achievements. With the magnificent conception of its north front (**116**), touched all too briefly by the morning or evening sun, it can also be taken as a powerful summary of Vanbrugh's maturity. He was dealing again, as at King's Weston and Lumley, with a son succeeding at his father's death. On 30 July 1723 Vanbrugh informed the Duke of Newcastle 'That my Old Friend & Ally The Great Chamberlain is at last, gone.' This was the 1st Duke of Ancaster, and a further letter of 20 August[72] to the Duke noted that after he had done 'Swigging' the waters at Scarborough, he was to call on 'his new Grace of Ancaster ... to consult about his Building; by which I believe he is inclin'd to go on upon the General Design I made for his Father last Winter and which was approv'd of by himself.'

Vanbrugh had visited the medieval house of Grimsthorpe at least once

in earlier years. In December 1718, detouring on his way to spend Christmas at Castle Howard, he carried a letter from London to the 1st Duke
of Ancaster.[73] A little of what he had to do when building up the new
north front may be gained from viewing the attractive range of buildings
to the south – the hipped roof and dormers are of the 1680s – or the way
the north towers are cut in to the east and west fronts (**117**). Early in
1724 Vanbrugh was laid up 'on Account of the Distemper', and took a
later opportunity to spend most of a month recuperating, in July–August,
at Castle Howard and Scarborough. He may have taken the opportunity
of being in the north to visit Grimsthorpe, as he did Seaton Delaval, but
there is only confirmation of the last, in a letter of 23 August 1724 to the
Duke of Newcastle.[74] In any case money and enthusiasm at Grimsthorpe
seem to have run out at Vanbrugh's death. According to the inscriptions
to the plates in Campbell's *Vitruvius Britannicus* (**113-114**), it was intended
to rebuild the entire house. The Garden front engraving (**114**) is even
doubtfully inscribed as a Vanbrugh design, but nothing was done.

The central block (**116**) has the massive grandeur of a Roman amphitheatre, with its two tiers of arched windows. These are flanked by great
banded Tuscan coupled columns, which, with the square-cut pilasters
behind them seem to be cutting through the wall in one powerful movement. It is pointless to speculate on the similar use of a rustic but Ionic
order on Palladio's Villa Sarego (*c* 1569), but a study for it had appeared
in his *Quattro Libri*. He may have also talked to the Huguenot Nicholas
Dubois, who had translated Leoni's *Palladio* in 1715, and who had been
appointed master-mason to the Board of Works in November 1719. What
is more to the point is that the effect, however derived, was given further
impact by the great blocks atop the columns, supporting two statuary
Rape groups. Above the balustrade, with its four urns, are the Ancaster
arms on a true Vanbrughian scale. The doorway does not now match
what Vanbrugh intended – comparison with an early drawing (**112**) is
informative – and the great brackets dying into the front below it, which
are shown thereon, would have been preferable to correct Doric trimmings.

The forecourt is in Vanbrugh's original conception (plan, **115**), and is
bound to east and west by walls of 26 bays of rusticated niches, linked to
two-storey pavilions (**116**). These repeat the main towers on the north
front, cut as sharply, in Ancaster stone, quarried in the park. Connecting
them is Thomas Warren's screen and gates,[75] showing motifs which have
been noted in his work elsewhere. Warren had also worked for Vanbrugh
at Blenheim, and (on stylistic evidence) at Kimbolton.

Within the house we are given the finest of all Vanbrugh's rooms, the
Great Hall (**118, 120**), which echoes the external treatment, with two
storeys of arcading. The north wall has seven bays of windows, as can be
seen, obviously, in an exterior view (**116**): that to the south has grisaille

paintings of seven English kings by Sir James Thornhill (**118, 120**). It is
on the west and east sides however that the spatial *bravura* comes through:
triplets of arched openings through which can be seen Thomas Warren's
superb staircase balustrades (**121**). The ceiling, the rich black and cream
patterned marble floor, and the arcades have all the correct curves to give
an overwhelming unity. The effect might have been richer still had the
concave oval centre of the ceiling been painted – it was intended surely?
– but Thornhill missed here an opportunity to advance his art. Vanbrugh's death was probably a contributory cause, but the house has a
number of traits that indicate Hawksmoor may have carried it forward.[76]
This however may be a theory that denies to Vanbrugh some of the credit
for a 'brilliant improvisation[77], which he was at least able to carry through
on the north front. There was a concern there to see that the best was
built for one whose father, the 1st Duke, had stood a year or two before
as godfather to John and Henrietta Maria's young son, the newly named
'John Vanbrugh' (**2**). But neither John, nor his illustrious architect father,
lived long enough to enjoy a long stay in a house which he had made, as
Arthur Young wrote in 1768, 'extremely magnificent'.[78]

CHRONOLOGY

ABBREVIATIONS

JV   John Vanbrugh

Webb, *Letters*   *The Complete Works of Sir John Vanbrugh: Vol. IV, The Letters*, ed. Geoffrey Webb (1928).

24 January 1664   J. V. born in the parish of St Nicholas Acons, City of London, to Giles van Brugg, merchant from Haarlem, and Elizabeth, youngest daughter of Sir Dudley Carleton, Imber Court, Surrey.

1667   Vanbrugh family moved to Chester, where Giles managed a sugar-refining and confectionery business.

1681   J. V. worked in London for his cousin, William Matthews, a wine merchant.

30 January 1686   J. V. commissioned as Captain in Earl of Huntingdon's Foot Regiment, but resigned during the summer.

16 September 1687   J. V. Bailiff in the retinue of James Bertie, Earl of Abingdon, High Steward of Oxford. Removed from office by order of King James II, February 1688.

Late summer 1688   Arrested in France for talking about William of Orange; imprisoned, latterly in the Bastille.

July 1689   Giles Vanbrugh, J. V.'s father, died.

April 1693   J. V. finally released from prison: returned from France to England.

May 1693   J. V. took up post of Auditor for the Southern Division of the Duchy of Lancaster (relinquished post in 1702).

1695   J. V. commissioned as Captain of Marines. Regiment was disbanded in 1698.

26 December 1696   J. V. staged his first play, *The Relapse, or Virtue in Danger.*

Spring 1697   J. V. staged his second play *Aesop.*

May 1697   J. V. staged *The Provok'd Wife.*

March 1698   Jeremy Collier published criticisms of J. V.'s dramatic works in his *Short View of the Immorality and Profaneness of the English Stage.*

June 1698   J. V. published *A Short Vindication of the Provok'd Wife and The Relapse from Immorality and Profaneness.*

1699   J. V. supplanted William Talman as architect to the 3rd Earl of Carlisle, and prepared plans for Castle Howard.

J. V. travelled during the summer to see 'most of the great houses in the North' (Webb, *Letters*, p. 4). Indicated (December) that a model for Castle Howard was in preparation, to be shown to the King at Kensington.

March 1700   J. V. produced his version of Beaumont and Fletcher's *The Pilgrims.*

1700–1   J. V. built 'Goose Pie House' in Whitehall for himself. (Demolished 1898).

January 1701   J. V. produced *The False Friend.*

Spring 1701   Work began at Castle Howard.

1702   J. V. resigned from the Army on his appointment as Comptroller (below).

June 1702	J.V. succeeded William Talman as Comptroller of His Majesty's Works.	September 1706	The 1st Earl of Godolphin wrote of Blenheim: 'The building is so far advanc'd that one may see perfectly how it will be when it is done.' Gardens in progress (under J.V.'s supervision) by Henry Wise.
1703	With William Congreve and Thomas Betterton J.V. set up a scheme for a new theatre in the Haymarket. J.V. appointed to Board of Directors of Greenwich Hospital.	1707	Blenheim Bridge being built (see **66–67**). East wing of house to cornice level.
June 1703	J.V. produced *The Country House*.	1707–8	J.V. leased the Haymarket Theatre to Owen McSwiny. J.V. to Earl of Manchester, 1708, 11 May 'I have parted with my whole concern to Mr Swiney; only reserving my Rent . . .'. (Webb, *Letters*, p. 20).
21 June 1703	J.V. appointed as Carlisle Herald in the College of Arms.		
March 1704	J.V. appointed Clarenceux Herald.		
18 April 1704	Foundation stone of the Haymarket Opera House laid by Lady Sunderland. Work proceeded on the building during 1704 and Spring 1705.	1708	J.V. built Screen and two-flight staircase at Audley End, Essex (see **82**); J.V. involved in rebuilding Kimbolton for the Earl (later 1st Duke) of Manchester. Gave advice in 1707, house completed 1710, with paintings by Pellegrini and Marco Ricci. Private apartments at Blenheim being decorated.
December 1704	J.V. and the 1st Duke of Marlborough chose the site for a house at Woodstock, and J.V. and Nicholas Hawksmoor began to plan its appearance and layout.		
18 January 1705	Queen Anne granted the Duke of Marlborough the estate of the Royal Manor of Woodstock, and indicated his house (the eventual Blenheim Palace) would be built as a thanks-offering by the nation for his military victories.	June 1709	J.V. quarrelled with Duchess of Marlborough over repairs to the Old Manor House at Woodstock. The main block at Blenheim almost ready for its roof.
April 1705	Model of Blenheim sent to Kensington for Queen Anne's approval.	November 1709	Pellegrini and Marco Ricci began painting at Castle Howard (High Saloon, Garden Room, Hall (pendentives and Dome). Completed their work by September 1712 (see **33**). J.V. built his house, Chargate, near Esher, Surrey (see **83**).
9 April 1705	First performance at the Haymarket Opera House.		
18 June 1705	Foundation stone of Blenheim Palace laid. J.V. appointed its Surveyor.		
October 1705	J.V. produced *The Confederacy*.	October 1710	Sarah, Duchess of Marlborough stopped all work at Blenheim. However, by December £7000 had been obtained from the Treasury, and work resumed on the decoration of Hall and Saloon.
November 1705	J.V. produced *The Mistake*.		
1706	J.V., as Clarenceux Herald, took the insignia of the Order of the Garter to the Elector of Hanover, (afterwards King George I). Castle Howard. Main block well advanced, East wing near completion.	1711	J.V. hoped to make the east wing of Blenheim 'ready for furniture' and hoped that paving in the Great Court and the steps up to the

Portico (see **46, 48**) might be done. J.V. appointed as a 'Commissioner for the building of Fifty New Churches in London'.

1712	Queen Anne stopped all Treasury money for building at Blenheim. The Duke and Duchess of Marlborough leave for the Continent. J.V. began work on King's Weston, Gloucs.
1713	J.V. dismissed as Comptroller of Her Majesty's Works. His patent was revoked 16 April, J.V. wrote to a relative on 2 April. 'I am turn'd out of my place in the Works for writing a Letter to the Mayor of Woodstock in which I say the Duke of Marlborough has been bitterly and barbarously persecuted' (Webb, *Letters*, p. 55).
1714	J.V. altered London house for the Duke of Newcastle.
August 1714	George I acceded to throne and the Duke of Marlborough and his Duchess returned from abroad.
19 September 1714	J.V. knighted.
November 1714	J.V. submitted design for Church of St Mary-le-Strand, London (not executed).
1715	J.V. reappointed Comptroller of His Majesty's Works, and (June) appointed 'Surveyor of Gardens and Waterworks belonging to the Royal Palaces'.
May 1715	J.V. submitted design for Church of St George, Bloomsbury (not executed). J.V. started certain interiors at Hampton Court for George, Prince of Wales. Completed 1718. J.V. appointed Garter King of Arms (to 1717 when position reverted to John Anstis). J.V. commenced alterations at Chargate which he had sold to the Duke of Newcastle (who renamed it Claremont).

	J.V. altered Walpole House, Chelsea for Sir Robert Walpole.
1716	J.V. appointed Surveyor at Greenwich Hospital.
April 1716	Work resumed at Blenheim. J.V. dealing with the Duke of Marlborough.
May 1716	The Duke has a stroke, J.V. dealing with Sarah, Duchess of Marlborough.
June 1716	The Duke and Duchess in residence, east wing of Blenheim.
1717	J.V. acquired land at Greenwich.
February 1718	Dated design for forecourt of King's Weston. J.V. built houses for himself and his brothers at Greenwich. J.V. started the building at Eastbury (see **68–79**).
August	J.V. paid his first visit to Seaton Delaval.
January 1719	J.V. aged 54, married at York to Henrietta Maria, daughter of Colonel James Yarburgh of Heslington Hall, York (she was born 1693, died 1776 – see below). A daughter was born to J.V. and his wife but died soon after. J.V. suggested alterations to Nottingham Castle (Webb, *Letters*, pp. 107–11) and completed a 'New Room' at Claremont, both for the Duke of Newcastle.
1720	A son, Charles, was born to J.V. and his wife; he died 1745 (see below). The office courts at Eastbury completed.
August 1721	J.V. inspected the work in progress at Seaton Delaval, and visited Lumley Castle to 'form a General Design for the whole' (Webb, *Letters*, p. 138).
November 1721	J.V. prepared part of his answer to the Chancery suit brought by the Duke of Marlborough 'against everybody concern'd in the Building at Blenheim' (Webb, *Letters*, p. 140).

January 1721-2	A son, John, was born to J. V. and his wife (he died in infancy in 1723).
16 June 1722	The Duke of Marlborough died at Windsor Lodge, aged 73 years. J. V. proposed a mausoleum at Blenheim, but the Duke had declared in his will that he should be buried in the Chapel to the house.
1722-5	Hawksmoor completed work at Blenheim Palace.
1723	The Duchess of Marlborough had the outworks at Blenheim finished. J. V. supervised amendments to the Prince's Rooms at Hampton Court.
August 1723	J. V. called on the 2nd Duke of Ancaster at Grimsthorpe to 'discuss the General Design I made for his Father last Winter' (Webb, Letters, p. 151).
February 1724	Work proceeded on the outworks at Castle Howard. The Temple of the Four Winds was under consideration. Work proceeded at Eastbury, according to J. V.'s Second Design (see **108-11**).
February 1725	J. V.'s design for the Castle Howard Temple approved by the Earl of Carlisle.
July–August 1725	J.V. undertook a six-week tour with his wife, and the Earl of Carlisle and his daughters. They visited Woodstock but by instruction of the Duchess of Marlborough J. V. and his wife were not allowed 'to see either House, Gardens, or even to enter the Park' at Blenheim (Webb, Letters, p. 167).
September 1725	J. V. received £1700 in fees due for his work at Blenheim: still owed £300 (Webb, Letters, p. 169).
26 March 1726	J. V. died at his house in Whitehall after a short illness. He was buried in the family vault at St Stephen Walbrook.
22 April 1726	J. V.'s will was proved. Hawksmoor continued work at Castle Howard (completed Temple; 1731), began erection of Mausoleum; completed after his death in 1736 (see below).
1728	Production of *The Provok'd Husband* by Cibber, incorporating J. V.'s unfinished *A Journey to London*.
25 March 1736	Hawksmoor (*b.* 1661) died at his house in Millbank, Westminster. Mausoleum at Castle Howard completed 1737-42, with balustraded steps and outer court by Daniel Garrett (?-1753).
1745	Charles Vanbrugh, J. V.'s son, killed at the Battle of Fontenoy.
26 April 1776	Lady Vanbrugh, J. V.'s widow, died at Greenwich, aged 82.

Note: A list of the occasions that Vanbrugh attended meetings of the Board of Works, 1715-1726, is given by Kerry Downes, *Vanbrugh* (1977) pp. 260-1.

NOTES

CHAPTER I

1. P. Smithers, *Life of Addison* (1968) p. 108.

2. Mark Noble. *The History of the College of Arms ...* (1804).

3. The Carleton, Vanbrugh, and related pedigrees are examined at length by Downes, Pt II, p. 127 *et seq.*

4. Tipping and Hussey, p. xiii. See also Downes, p. 15.

5. Downes, pp. 6–7, for 'Kinship in Vanbrugh's Patrons and Associates'.

6. The early years are described, stylishly, by Whistler (1938), pp. 16–22.

7. A. Rosenberg, 'New Light on Vanbrugh' (eight unpublished letters), *Philological Quarterly*, XLV (1966) pp. 603–13.

8. Downes, p. 16, fn. 16.

9. Dr S. Lang, reviewing Downes, *Journal, Society of Architectural Historians*, 38, Pt 2 (May 1979) pp. 108–10, and quoting Hist Mss. Comm., 78, Hastings II, p. 181.

10. Colvin, *King's Works* V (1976) p. 33.

11. Paul Hopkins, 'John Vanbrugh's imprisonment in France, 1688–93', *Notes and Queries* vol. 26 (1979) pp. 529–34; Frank McCormick, 'Vanbrugh's imprisonment in France: More Light', *ibid.*, vol. 29 (February 1982) pp. 57–61.

12. Downes, p. 16, fn. 22.

13. Sir John Summerson (reviewing David Green, *Blenheim Palace*) *The New Statesman and Nation*, 12 April, 1952, p. 438.

14. Downes, pp. 245–6.

15. *ibid.*, pp. 247–8.

16. *ibid.*, pp. 249–50.

17. R. J. Gordon, 'Vanbrugh at sea', *Notes and Queries*, 26 December 1979) pp. 526–9, citing Lord Carmarthen's *A Journal of the Brest-Expedition* (1694), (two copies in British Library, *cf.* Peregrine Osborne, 2nd Duke of Leeds, for catalogue entry).

18. For the conditions of the stage in Vanbrugh's day see W. B. van Lennep, *The London Stage, 1660–1800*, 2 vols, Carbondale (1960).

19. Whistler (1938) pp. 29–30. See also Judith Milhous, *Thomas Betterton and the management of Lincoln's Inn Fields, 1695–1708*, Carbondale, Southern Illinois Univ. Press (1979).

20. Whistler (1938) pp. 42–3; see also A. Williams writing in *Publns. Modern Language Association* 90 (1975) pp. 234–46.

21. *ibid.*, (1938) p. 106.

22. Downes, p. 43, gives a conjectural reconstruction of the theatre as built, and after the 1708 alterations. See also Bibliography for listing of articles by Milhous, Mullin and Olleson.

23. Webb, *Letters*, pp. 20–1.

24. *ibid.*, p. 24.

25. Nicholas Rowe, 'The 'Reconcilement between Jacob Tonson and Mr Congreve', *Works* (1757), includes:

    I'm in with Captain Vanbrugh at the present,
    A most SWEET-NATURED gentleman, and pleasant;
    He writes your comedies, draws schemes, and models,
    And builds duke's houses upon very odd hills:
    For him, so much I dote on him, that I,
    If I was sure to go to heaven, would die.

26. Bonamy Dobrée, *English Literature in the Early Eighteenth Century* (1964) p. 231.

27. See Bibliography for a note on the annual listing of literary research about Vanbrugh, and modern editions of his plays.

28. Printed by Whistler (1938), Appendix 4; Harold Williams, *The Poems of Jonathan Swift*, 2nd edn., (1958) vol. 1, pp. 78, 85.

29. John Summerson, *Architecture in Britain 1530–1830*, 5th revd. edn. (1969) pp. 166–7; Vanbrugh as a 'brilliant novice' *cf.*, Colvin, *King's Works*, V, p. 36.

30. *ibid.*, p. 36.

31. A. R. Wagner, *Heralds of England* (1967). For some of Vanbrugh's papers as a Herald, see Bibliography: Manuscript Sources, and the entry under J. Milhous in Appendix A.

32. Whistler, p. 241.

33. Webb, *Letters*, p. 123.

34. H. M. Colvin, 'The Fifty New Churches', *Architectural Review*, CVII, March 1950, pp. 189–96; E. G. W. Bill, ed., *The Queen Anne Churches: A Catalogue of Papers ... for Building Fifty New Churches ...* (1979), with introduction by H. M. Colvin; Kerry Downes, *Hawksmoor* (1969) pp. 156–99.

35. S. Lang, 'Vanbrugh's Theory and Hawksmoor's Buildings', *Journal, Society of Architectural Historians*, XXIV (1965) pp. 127–51, but her conclusions are questioned by Downes in his *Hawksmoor* (1969), and *Vanbrugh* (1977).

36. Terry Friedman, *James Gibbs* (1984) p. 325.

37. Bodleian Library, Oxford, MS. Rawl., B. 376, f. 351, printed by Whistler, pp. 247–52, and Downes, pp. 257–8.

38. Whistler, p. 252.

39. Webb, *Letters*, p. 53.

40. *ibid.*, p. 60.

41. Colvin, *King's Works*, V, p. 55.

42. Downes, Appendix G.

43. Webb, *Letters*, pp. 96, 104; Whistler, pp. 244–5.

44. Colvin, *King's Works*, V, p. 56.

45. Webb, *Letters*, p. 98.

46. Colvin, *op. cit.*, pp. 58–9.

47. Colvin, *op. cit.*, pp. 62–5.

48. Colvin, *Dictionary*, p. 416.

49. Webb, *Letters*, p. 115.

50. This can be determined from the *Calendar of Treasury Books*, VII, Pt. 3, pp. 1483, 1523; VIII, Pt. 2, pp. 1054, 1094, 1118; XVII, Pt. 1, pp. 254, 271, 369; Burke's *Landed Gentry* (1853) vol. II, p. 1665; Henry Snyder, ed., *The Marlborough-Godolphin Correspondence*, vol. 3 (1975) p. 1479, fn. 4.

51. J. Foster, *Pedigrees of the Country Families of York* (1874); Burke's *Landed Gentry* (1853) vol. II, p. 1665. Heslington Hall was acquired by the Morrell Trust from the 5th Lord Deramore, and deeded to the new University of York (1960).

52. Downes, p. 98, fn. 20, and in *Burlington Magazine*, vol. 124 (March 1982) pp. 153–5. Dobrée, *Works*, I, p. xxxii is in error in assuming Vanbrugh's first love was Henrietta Maria, or her mother, Anne, who died in 1718.

53. Leeds Archives Dept., Studley Royal MSS., letters 13151, 13740, first published by Geoffrey Beard, *Georgian Craftsmen and their Work* (1966) p. 53.

54. L. O. J. Boynton on Baldersby, in H. Colvin and J. Harris, eds., *The Country Seat* (1970) pp. 97–105.

55. Whistler (1938) p. 251.

56. Webb, *Letters*, pp. 110–111.

57. *ibid.*, p. 111–112.

58. *ibid.*, p. 116.

59. *ibid.*, p. 120.

60. Whistler (1938) p. 257 is in error giving the date as 12 May 1719. See **2** for the family Bible inscription recording 'Born Oct^br 20th, 1720'.

61. Webb, *Letters*, p. 126.

62. *ibid.*, p. 133.

63. *ibid.*, pp. 136–7.

64. Not 'February, 1722' as noted by Downes, p. 97, if we assume that Henrietta recorded the birthday of her son (14 January) correctly in the family Bible (**2**). However the midwife was paid on February 14 according to the entry in Vanbrugh's account-book (Downes, p. 213, fn. 276), so the possibility cannot be discounted.

65. Webb, *Letters*, p. 147.

66. These can be established by payments to physicians in his account-book published by Downes, one page of which is illustrated here (**5**).

67. *ibid.*, p. 172.

68. Whistler, *repr.*, p. 252, from Rigaud's view of 1734.

69. Suggested by Frank McCormick in 'The embattled career of Sir John Vanbrugh', University of Minnesota thesis, 1977, summarised in *Dissertation Abstracts*, 39, 901A; and further in his article on Vanbrugh's imprisonment in France, in *Notes and Queries*, 29 (February 1982) pp. 57–61.

CHAPTER II

1. Webb, *Letters*, pp. 4–5.

2. For the manorial descent see *Victoria County History of Yorkshire* (*N. Riding*), Vol. 2, pp. 110–111.

3. Whistler, p. 27.

4. John Harris, *William Talman: Maverick Architect* (1984).

5. Whistler, Figs. 21 and 22.

6. First printed in *Country Life*, 30 January 1953, and then by Whistler, pp. 35, 229.

7. Sotheby's, May 23, 1951. Collection of the Marquess of Bute.

8. Webb, *Letters*, pp. 56–7.

9. Webb, *Letters*, pp. 6–7.

10. Colvin, *Dictionary*, p. 402.

11. D. J. Watkin, ed., *Sale Catalogues of Libraries of Eminent Persons*, vol. 4 (1972) pp. 45–106.

12. Webb, *Letters*, p. 4 '... I have been this Summer at my Ld. Carlisle's, and Seen most of the great houses in the North ... I stay'd at Chattesworth four or five days the Duke being there ...'.

13. Geoffrey Beard, *Decorative Plasterwork in Great Britain* (1975) p. 54.

14. Tipping and Hussey, pp. 23–6; *Burlington Magazine*, Vol. 78 (1941) pp. 3–9; *The Times*, 11 November 1940.

15. Downes, pp. 37–8, 44–5; notably by Charles Saumarez-Smith, in his Cambridge Ph.D. Thesis, on the 3rd Earl of Carlisle, Ch. V.

16. Webb, *Letters*, p. 161.

17. Whistler, *op. cit.*, pp. 48–50; Geoffrey Webb, 'The Letters and Drawings ... relating to ... the Mausoleum at Castle Howard', *Walpole Society*, XIX (1931).

18. Castle Howard, 3rd Earl's Disbursement Book 'Total disbursed in my Buildings, gardens, plantations & out works to Mids. 1737. £78,240. 2s. 10d.'

19. Blenheim cost £287,000, David Green, *Blenheim Palace* (1951) p. 137.

20. David Green, *Sarah, Duchess of Marlborough* (1967) p. 98.

21. James Craggs, Snr. (1657–1721) acted for a time as the Marlborough household's business manager, having attracted the attention of the Duchess by 'his shrewdness and administrative ability' – cf. *Dictionary of National Biography* for his career, as Postmaster-General, Member of Parliament, *et. al.*

22. Green, *Sarah, Duchess, op. cit.*, p. 105.

23. Green, *Blenheim*, p. 50.

24. Vanbrugh wrote to Lord Poulett on 30 September 1710 (Webb, *Letters*, p. 45) and stated that 'A very large, Exact, and intelligible Model of the Building, was made in wood and when it was compleated it was set in the Gallery at Kensington by her [the Queen's] Order, and there left sometime, that she might Consider it at her leisure, both Alone, and with other people ... She Expressed her Self extreamly Pleasd with it ...'.

25. Green, *Blenheim*, p. 50 quotes William Upcott's *Diary* as recording that the stone was struck by Sir Thomas Wheate of Glympton, whose quarries were providing stone, Dr Bouchell, and Vanbrugh (as third) – 'I know not the rest' Upcott wrote. Green, *ibid.*, p. 327 indicates that Hawksmoor was present, as one would expect, and Vanbrugh informed the Duke the stone had been laid in a letter dated June 22, 1705, the same week as the ceremony (18 June 1705) (Green, *ibid.*, p. 55).

26. Green, *Blenheim*, p. 59 lists the quarries and shows their geographical position in relation to Blenheim.

27. Webb, *Letters*, p. 45.

28. *The New Statesman and Nation*, 12 April 1952, p. 438.

29. David Green, *Henry Wise, Gardener to Queen Anne*, Oxford (1956).

30 Green, *Blenheim*, p. 85, citing British Library, MS., 19,606.

31. Webb, *Letters*, p. 14.

32. Webb, *Letters*, p. 215.

33. Deposited in the British Library, with other Blenheim manuscripts, in 1980. (B. L. Add. MS., 61353, ff. 62–67b., autograph, and other copies).

34. Webb, *Letters*, p. 28.

35. Webb, *Letters*, p. 29.

36. Edward Gregg, *Queen Anne* (1980) pp. 315, 319.

37. Gilbert Burnet, *History of His Own Time*, VI, (1833) p. 35.

38. Gregg, *op. cit.*, p. 329.

39. Green, *Blenheim*, p. 109, citing the Duchess's letter of 4 December 1710.

40. Winston Churchill, *Marlborough, His Life and Times* (1947 edn.) II, p. 912.

41. Webb, *Letters*, p. 60.

42. Gregg, *op. cit.*, p. 375.

43. Gregg, *op. cit.*, p. 391.

44. Webb, *Letters*, p. 89, but incorrectly stated as addressed to 'Lord Godolphin' instead of 'Lord Carlisle'.

45. *Whistler*, p. 243.

46. Harriett was the daughter of Henrietta, 2nd Duchess of Marlborough, (1681–1733), through her marriage to Francis, 2nd Earl of Godolphin.

47. Webb, *Letters*, p. 90.

48. Green, *Sarah, Duchess, op. cit.*, p. 203.

49. Webb, *Letters*, pp. 84–5.

50. Green, *Blenheim*, pl. 68. See the papers in British Library, Add MS., 61355, Vol. CCLV, ff. 18–.

51. Webb, *Letters*, p. 130.

52. Webb, *Letters*, Appendix I (p. 177, *et seq.*).

53. British Library, Add MS., 19, 611.

54. Green, *Blenheim*, p. 152, citing British Library, Add MS., 19,614; for papers relating to the law-suits see also British Library, Add MS., 61356.

55. Webb, *Letters*, p. 135.

56. The papers relating to the removal of the Duke's body to London, and many years later (1744) to the chapel at Blenheim are in British Library, Add MS., 61409, ff. 20–22b; 61410.

57. Webb, *Letters*, p. 138.

58. Green, *Blenheim*, p. 264, quoting a letter of the Duchess in December 1715, of which the location is now unknown.

59. British Library, Add MS., 38056.

60. Webb, *Letters*, p. 146 (Vanbrugh to Jacob Tonson, 18 June 1722).

61. Webb, *Letters*, p. 148.
62. Green, *Blenheim*, p. 316.

CHAPTER III

1. Webb, *Letters*, p. 13.
2. *ibid.*, p. 24.
3. The Saloon is illustrated by Tipping and Hussey, pls. 158-9.
4. Webb, *Letters*, p. 19.
5. *ibid.*, p. 26.
6. Edward Croft-Murray, *Decorative Painting in England* (1962) I, p. 14, Pl. 3.
7. Whistler, p. 199.
8. *ibid.*, p. 144.
9. Whistler, pp. 144-5; Colvin, *Dictionary*, p. 147.
10. Tipping and Hussey, *repr.*, p. 174.
11. *ibid.*, p. 174.
12. *Dictionary of National Biography*.
13. Webb, *Letters*, p. 55.
14. Kerry Downes, 'The King's Weston Book of Drawings', *Architectural History*, 10 (1967) pp. 9-88.
15. C. Gotch, 'Mylne and King's Weston', *Country Life*, 23 January 1953, pp. 212-5.
16. Tipping and Hussey, Pl. 186; Kerry Downes, *Hawksmoor*, 2nd edn. (1979) Pl. 8.
17. Tipping and Hussey, Pl. 211; Downes, *Architectural History*, *op. cit.*, fig. 17.
18. S. Lang, 'Vanbrugh's Theory and Hawksmoor's Buildings', *Journal, Society of Architectural Historians*, XXIV (1965) p. 135.
19. Whistler, pp. 200-3; Downes, pp. 93-7 (with plan of site, and houses).
20. Downes, p. 100.
21. Robert Wark, ed., *Sir Joshua Reynolds, Discourses on Art*, Huntington Library, Calif., (1959) p. 244.
22. *London Topographical Society Record* IV (1907); *Greenwich Antiquarian Soc.*, I. 3. (1912), *repr.* in Tipping and Hussey, p. 191; Downes, pls. 102-114.
23. Webb, *Letters*, p. 61.
24. Geoffrey Beard, *Craftsmen and Interior Decoration in England, 1660-1820* (1981) p. 287.
25. Webb, *Letters*, p. 63.
26. C. G. T. Dean, *The Royal Hospital, Chelsea* (1950) pp. 202-3.
27. Webb, *Letters*, p. 88.
28. Beard, *op. cit.*, pp. 265, 284.
29. Webb, *Letters*, p. xxviii.
30. Whistler, pl. 57 (Rocque); Downes, pl. 118 (Rigaud).
31. N. B. Pevsner, *Buildings of England: Nottinghamshire* (1951) p. 130.

32. Webb, *Letters*, p. 105. The letter is British Library, Add MS., 33065, Vol. I, f. 169.
33. *ibid.*, p. 107.
34. *ibid.*, p. 110.
35. *ibid.*, p. 82, dated November as 1716; Downes, p. 80, fn 9 notes the letter has an endorsement for 1 November, 1723.
36. Downes, p. 118, fn 20.
37. Tipping and Hussey, p. 175.
38. Peter Willis, *Charles Bridgeman* (1977) p. 47.
39. Whistler, p. 157.
40. *ibid.*, Pls. 62-3.
41. Tipping and Hussey, p. 176, suggested Campbell's plan (**71**) had been reversed in engraving, but Whistler, p. 161 disputed this. It seems therefore to be part of the stable block, to the west, which survives (**76**).
42. For a fuller account of Eastbury than can be given here see Tipping and Hussey, Ch VIII, and Whistler, Ch VI.
43. Whistler, p. 161.
44. *ibid.*, p. 162, Pl. 71.
45. *ibid.*, p. 163, fn 2.
46. *ibid.*, pls. 74-5.
47. Tipping and Hussey, pl. 261.
48. Willis, *op. cit.*, p. 129, citing Daniel Defoe's tour of 1724-6.
49. Downes, p. 118.
50. Whistler, p. 171.
51. George Clarke, The History of Stowe - VII, 'The Vanbrugh - Bridgeman Gardens', *Stoic*, XXIII, July 1969, p. 257.
52. Webb, *Letters*. p. 112.
53. Willis, *op. cit.*, Ch 5, pls. 111-159, and especially pls. 123-8.
54. *ibid.*, p. 109, fn 14.
55. L. Whistler, M. Gibbon, G. Clarke, *Stowe: A Guide to the Gardens*, revd. edn., (1968) p. 13.
56. Clarke, *op. cit.*, p. 263.
57. Willis, *op. cit.*, pls. 116-7.
58. *ibid.*, p. 112.
59. Webb, *Letters*, p. 167.
60. *ibid.*, p. 168 (September 4, 1725, to the Earl of Carlisle).
61. Tipping and Hussey, p. 278. The Admiral's letter to Sir John Delaval, 23 January 1717 is displayed at Seaton Delaval (case 3).
62. Webb, *Letters*, pp. 137-8.
63. Geoffrey Beard, *Georgian Craftsmen and their Work* (1966) p. 52.
64. L. O. J. Boynton in *The Country Seat*, ed., H. M. Colvin and J. Harris (1970) pp. 97-105.

65. Lang, *op. cit.*, (n. 18 above), p. 138.
66. Webb, *Letters*, pp. 9, 236; Downes, p. 189, fn 110.
67. Seaton Delaval, Displays, Case 3.
68. Northumberland County Record Office (NRO.650), including (NRO.650/E/1) quarry accounts, payments to labourers, 1720-4. Some papers were also transferred there from the City Library (IDE.13/1-16), including a further letter (IDE.13/6) from James Mewburn of Newcastle to Admiral Delaval, December 10, 1720, saying he was enclosing Vanbrugh's design for the 'East Stare Case, that is for the East Tower'. This has not been traced, nor the letter mentioned at the end of Mewburn's letter, 'Inclosed a letter of Sr John Vanbrughs which I found this week. have taken a Copy of it'.
69. *ibid.*, IDE.13/11.
70. *ibid.*, IDE.13/12, Half yearly account for the building of Seaton Delaval Hall, ending 6 April 1729; for planting, ending 5 April 1729 (IDE.13/13).
71. Webb, *Letters*, pp. 137-8.
72. *ibid.*, pp. 150-1.
73. *ibid.*, pp. 105, 107-8.
74. *ibid.*, p. 161.
75. For a note about Warren's work at Grimsthorpe see that to pl. 165.
76. Downes, p. 121.
77. H. M. Colvin, 'Grimsthorpe Castle, the North Front' in Colvin and Harris, eds., *The Country Seat* (1970) pp. 91-3.
78. Arthur Young, *Tour through the North of England* (1768).

NOTE ON THE ILLUSTRATIONS

All photographs are by Anthony Kersting, F.R.P.S., unless otherwise stated

Cross references to each are given as appropriate. Measurements are given both in metres, and feet and inches. Notes on the references in the illustrations are to be found on pp. 167-8.

ILLUSTRATIONS

1. SIR JOHN VANBRUGH, 1664–1726, painting, attributed to Thomas Murray, oil on canvas, 90.2 × 69.9 cm (35½ × 27½ in), c 1718 *National Portrait Gallery, London*, No. 1568 (Photograph: Gallery).

Thomas Murray (1663–1735) painted in the Kneller style, but he had been a pupil of John Riley, Kneller's partner as 'Principal Painter' after the Revolution.

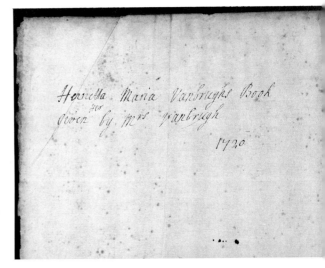

2. VANBRUGH FAMILY BIBLE and Book of Common Prayer. Printed by Thomas and John Buck, Printers to the University, Cambridge 1629 (Lady Mowbray and Stourton).

This Bible belonged to Elizabeth Vanbrugh, Sir John's mother. In 1720 she gave it to Henrietta Maria, Sir John's wife who records the gift, and further records the birth of their two sons, Charles and John. The interesting fact is the status of the godparents. In Charles's case these were Henrietta, Duchess of Marlborough, the 3rd Earl of Carlisle and Colonel James Yarburgh, and for John, Henrietta, Duchess of Newcastle, the 1st Duke of Ancaster and Viscount Cobham. The latter name is noted in Vanbrugh's account-book (Downes, p. 97 fn 14).

3. THE 'GOOSE-PIE HOUSE', Whitehall, London, 1700.
Drawing, pen, ink and coloured wash, made for Sir John
Soane, *c* 1803. *Sir John Soane's Museum, London* (Photograph: Museum).

On July 22, 1700 Lord Jersey wrote a letter to Sir
Christopher Wren: 'His Majty having granted leave to
John Vanbrugh Esq, to build himself a lodging in Whitehall ... and to allow him to make use of such brick and
stone out ye Rubbesh ...'. The 'rubbish' arose from the
fire of January 1698 which had devastated the greater
part of Whitehall Palace. Sir John Summerson has spe-
culated what service Vanbrugh may have rendered the
Crown for such a signal privilege, as the order was later
confirmed to the dubious Wren by the King's order.

The house, red brick with stone quoins, had good
views of the curving river and of the Banqueting House.
It survived until its demolition in 1895. The best view of
it now available was made for Sir John Soane in the
early nineteenth century. The two wings shown are a
later addition and the building was also given an iron
balcony and a coat of rusticated stucco. The building led
to the famous verse by Jonathan Swift (see p. 20), but
it provided Vanbrugh with a small house in the centre
of court circles, from which he could launch a second
career.

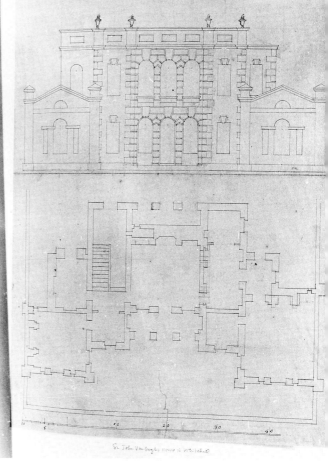

4. WHITEHALL Sir John Vanbrugh's House, Elevation
and Plan, ink on paper. *Sir Richard Proby, Bt* (Photograph: Courtauld Institute of Art).

For a note on Vanbrugh's 'Goose-Pie' House, as Jonathan Swift called it, see that to **3.**

81

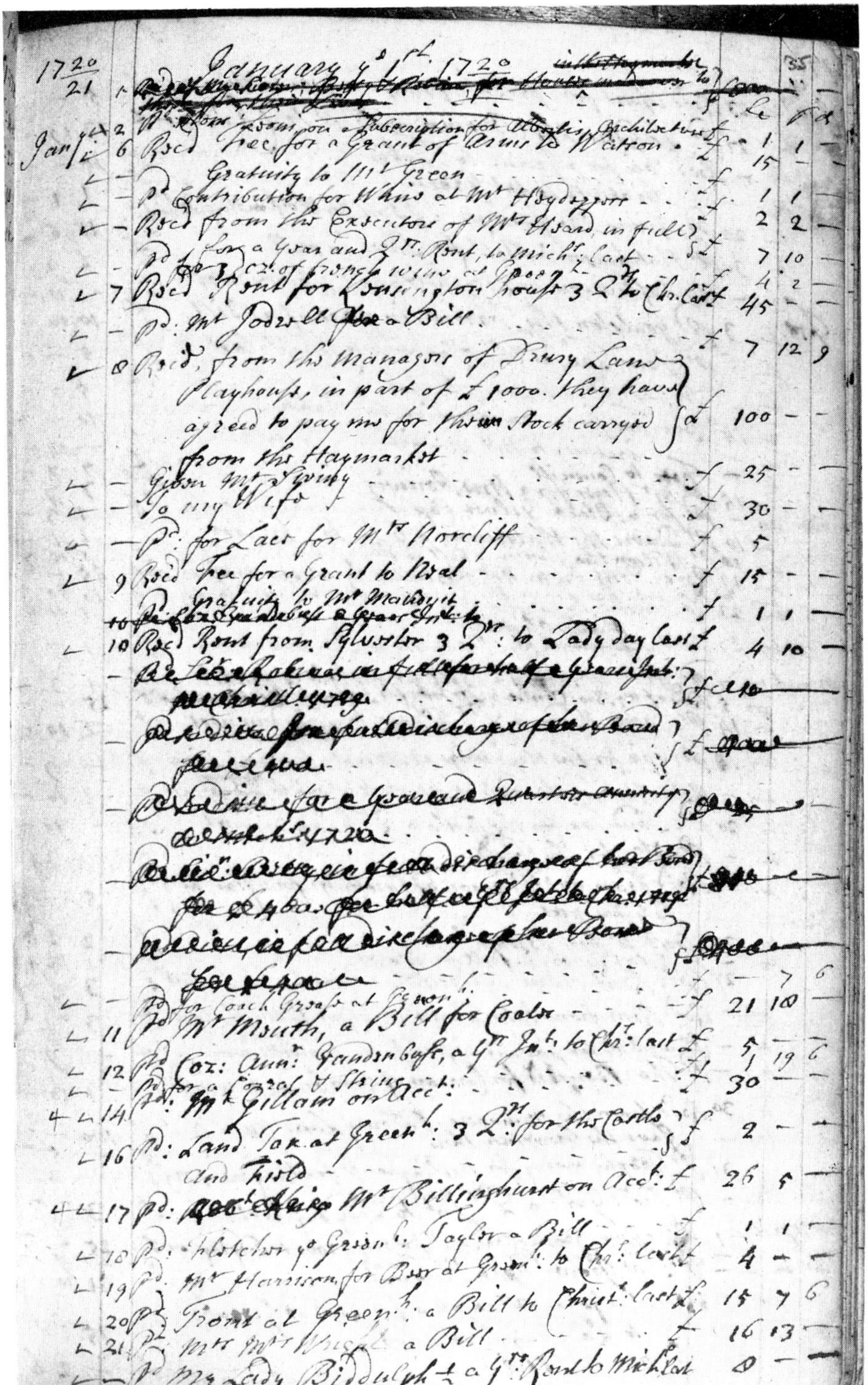

1720/21 January 1st. 1720

Jan. 2 [illegible] Subscription for [illegible] Architecture £ 1 1

6 Rec'd Fee for a Grant of Arms to Watson £ 15

Gratuity to Mr Green

Pd. Contribution for Whist at Mr Heydegger £ 1 1

Rec'd from the Executors of Mrs Hoard in full for a Year and Qr. Rent to Mich. last £ 2 2

Pd. for 3 ozs of french wine at Green. £ 7 10

7 Rec'd Rent for Kensington house 3 Qrs to Chr. last £ 4 2 / 45

Pd. Mr Jodrell for a Bill £ 7 12 9

8 Rec'd from the Managers of Drury Lane Playhouse, in part of £1000. they have agreed to pay me for their Stock carryed from the Haymarket £ 100

Given Mr Tuffnell £ 25

To my Wife £ 30

Pd. for Lace for Mrs Norcliff £ 5

9 Rec'd Fee for a Grant to Neal £ 15

Gratuity to Mr Maddox £ 1 1

10 Rec'd Rent from Sylvester 3 Qrs to Lady day last £ 4 10

[illegible]

Pd. for Coach Grass at Green. 7 6

Pd. Mr Mouth, a Bill for Coals £ 21 10

11 Pd. Cox: Ann: Vanderbuck, a Qr. Jnt. to Chr. last £ 5 19 6

12 Pd. for a Coral & String £ 30

14 Pd. Mr Gillam on Acct.

16 Pd. Land Tax at Green. 3 Qrs for the Castle and Field £ 2

17 Pd. Mr Billinghurst on Acct. £ 26 5

Pd. Fletcher ye Green. Taylor a Bill £ 1 1

18 Pd. Mr Harrison for Beer at Green. to Chr. last £ 4

19 Pd. Front at Green. a Bill to Christ. last £ 15 7 6

20 Pd. Mr Mrs Whistle a Bill £ 16 13

21 Pd. My Lady Biddulph ½ a Yr. Rent to Mich. last £ 8

5. SIR JOHN VANBRUGH'S ACCOUNT BOOK, entries for January 1721, folio 35 recto. Borthwick Institute of Historical Research, University of York (Photograph: University).

At the top of the entries Vanbrugh records his purchase of Giacomo Leoni's edition of Alberti's 'Architecture' at a cost of 1 guinea. He also notes his receipt of £100 as part-payment of £1000 due from the Managers of the Drury Lane Playhouse for stock transferred to them. Regrettably the account book does not start until 1715 and is therefore after Vanbrugh's work at Castle Howard and Blenheim. It was first published in 1977 by Downes.

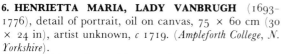

6. HENRIETTA MARIA, LADY VANBRUGH (1693-1776), detail of portrait, oil on canvas, 75 × 60 cm (30 × 24 in), artist unknown, c 1719. (*Ampleforth College, N. Yorkshire*).

Oral tradition allows this portrait to be considered as one of Henrietta Maria Yarburgh who married Vanbrugh in January, 1719. It was acquired for Ampleforth from the Deramore family, when they left Heslington Hall, near York, in 1958. A further portrait of Lady Vanbrugh, attributed to Isaac Whood, was reproduced in *The Connoisseur*, XLVIII (1917) p. 133 (*repr*: Downes **1**). Its present whereabouts is unknown.

7. CHARLES HOWARD, 3rd Earl of Carlisle (1669-1738), painting by Sir Godfrey Kneller, oil on canvas, 90 × 70 cm (35 × 27 in) c 1712, s., *National Portrait Gallery, London*, No. 3197 (Photograph: Gallery).

Lord Carlisle was a member of Parliament 1689-92, and held several court appointments during the reigns of Queen Anne and George I. Not only did he commission Vanbrugh to design Castle Howard for him, but used his considerable influence to advance the architect's career. In one of the early draft wills made many years before his death the Earl left bequests to Vanbrugh (who predeceased him by 12 years) and to Vanbrugh's clerk of works at Castle Howard, William Etty Jr., of York (d. 1734).

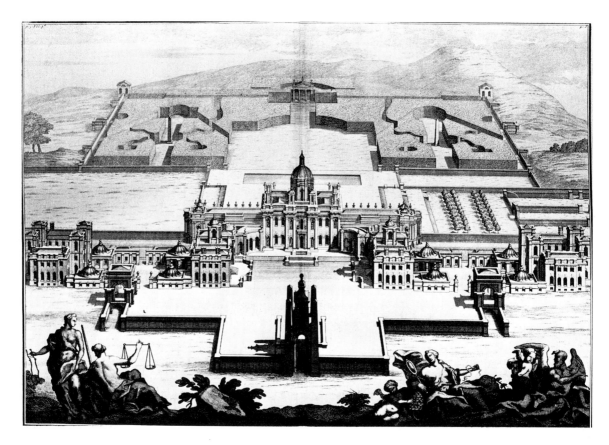

8. CASTLE HOWARD, Yorkshire. Bird's eye view from the north, Colen Campbell, *Vitruvius Britannicus*, III (1725), pls. 5-6 (Photograph: Birmingham Reference Library).

The engraving issued by Campbell was based on an elevation of 1717. A rough drawing for the layout by Vanbrugh is shown here (see **9**) but the published engraving may have been based on the work of Hawksmoor drawing it out.

The Great Obelisk Gate at the centre was mentioned frequently by Vanbrugh, who argued, alternately, for and against its provision. It was not built, but after his death a gateway was provided, which Hawksmoor did not like. The garden was laid out more or less as shown, but swept away in the late eighteenth century.

9. CASTLE HOWARD, Yorkshire, Sketch by Vanbrugh *c* 1718, ink on paper, *Victoria and Albert Museum, London,* No. D93–91 (Photograph: Museum).

This rough sketch by Vanbrugh was that probably worked up by Hawksmoor (?) for the bird's eye view of Castle Howard (see **8**) which was published in Colen Campbell's *Vitruvius Britannicus,* III, pl. 16 (1725). The two gateways to east and west (we are looking at the central block on the north side) appear to have been completed. That to the south – the Obelisk Gate – was worked on, and then abandoned. Vanbrugh wrote finally to Lord Carlisle on 10 December 1724: '... I don't think it wou'd be necessary (nor indeed proper) to have any opening there ...'

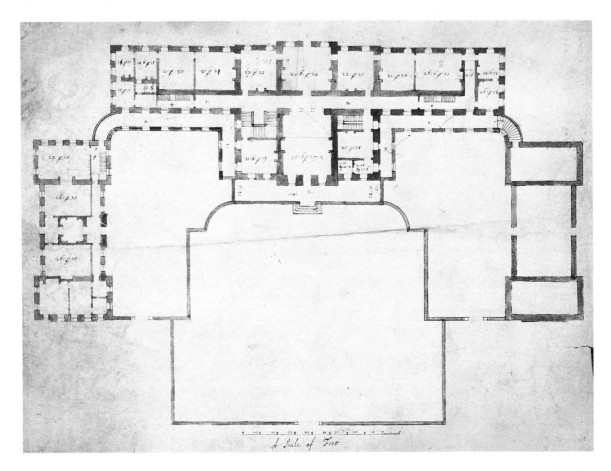

A Scale of Feett

10. CASTLE HOWARD, Yorkshire. First Plan, *c* 1699?, pen and ink on paper, *Victoria and Albert Museum, London*, (Photograph: Museum).

In 1951 a group of architectural drawings from the collection of Lord Bute were sold. Seventeen related to Castle Howard, and were presented, by the National Art Collections Fund, as part of a larger gift, to the Victoria & Albert Museum. This plan should be compared with the draft elevation formerly at Welbeck (see **15**). It enables the north front to be imagined entire, although there are still improvements to make before the elevations in *Vitruvius Britannicus* were engraved. The wings are 'weakly attached to the corners' of a shorter garden range. The hall is oblong, providing no base, as yet, for a great stone lantern, and the staircases were eventually modified.

In 1952 Sir John Summerson suggested (*The New Statesman and Nation*, 12 April 1952, p. 438) that the arrangement of Castle Howard was indebted to Sir Christopher Wren's 'First Scheme', perspective drawing, 1694 (repr. Geoffrey Beard, *The Work of Christopher Wren*, 1982, pl. 45), in the resemblance of dome and portico on the main axis with the curved colonnaded wings (see **11**). Laurence Whistler pointed out however that this early plan does not show that 'and therefore Greenwich was not the original inspiration'. Professor Downes has drawn attention to the well-managed colonnade at Wren's Chelsea Hospital, to which the Castle Howard preliminary south elevation is related (see **15**).

11. CASTLE HOWARD, Yorkshire. North Front, 1699–1706.

After it had been agreed that Vanbrugh should supplant William Talman as Lord Carlisle's architect he needed to check the site, agree rates with craftsmen, particularly the masons, prepare drawings and check the source of supplies, particularly stone. In these negotiations Hawksmoor's help in the precise arrangements that Vanbrugh had little heart for was invaluable. Quarries of good stone were opened in the park, and the masons, William Smith (in 1701) and John Ellsworth and Manger Smith (both 1703), were set to work. By the end of 1706 the centre block had received its entablature on all sides and the cupola was built. The stone carving really belongs in spirit to the work of William Talman at Chatsworth. During his short years of involvement the Huguenot carver Nadauld was there, and came on to Castle Howard to provide almost identical motifs on the south pediment (see **27**).

12. CASTLE HOWARD, Yorkshire. North Front, main block, 1699–1706.
For a note on the North Front see that to **11**.

13-14. CASTLE HOWARD, Yorkshire. Elevations, pen, ink and wash on paper. **13** 'First Proposal; Main Block, North Entrance Front; **14** 'Second Proposal; revised version, North Entrance Front. *Victoria & Albert Museum, London*, Nos. E426, 1951; E425, 1951 (Photographs: Museum).
The soldier-architect – for Vanbrugh had hardly left his military career when he started on the grand conception

– is here (1699–1700) revising the entrance front drawings. With Hawksmoor's experience and help the ornament, window openings and rustication was balanced, various window openings (especially over the front door) were tried, and modified again, before the facade was finally built (see **11, 12**). There is as yet no hint of the dome and lantern.

15. CASTLE HOWARD, Yorkshire. Preliminary Elevation, South Front, by Nicholas Hawksmoor, *c* 1702, inscr. on verso: 'Mr Vanbrooks draft of a great house' (the word *great* has been inserted). *Royal Institute of British Architects* (Photograph: R.I.B.A.).
This preliminary elevation incorporates a Dome, but still has some considerable differences from what was finally built (see **21**). The arrangement of the connecting corridors meant the occupant had no covered access into the distant wings and the central block was small with a dominant entablature. On grounds of convenience and appearance amendment was necessary.

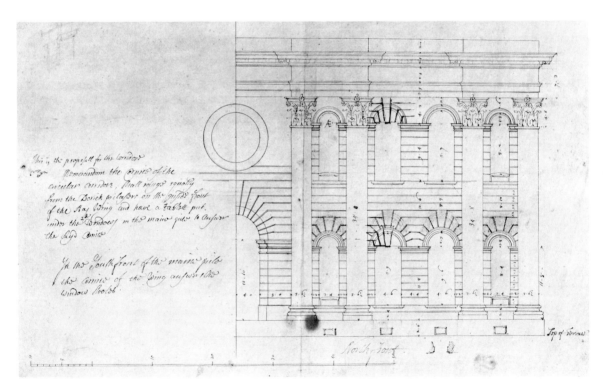

16. CASTLE HOWARD, Yorkshire. 'Second Proposal'; North Front, Main Block, *c* 1700 *Victoria and Albert Museum, London*, No. E424, 1951 (Photograph: Museum). Hawksmoor added a note to this spirited essay in rusticating a facade about the curved arcades, or corridors which finally became a dominant feature of the north front (see **11**). A circular window is being tried over the entrance door, and this feature was retained in a revision of the 'Second Proposal' (see **14**) which stands midway between the 'First Proposal' (see **13**) and the one finally published in *Vitruvius Britannicus*, to which the facade more or less approximates (see **1**).

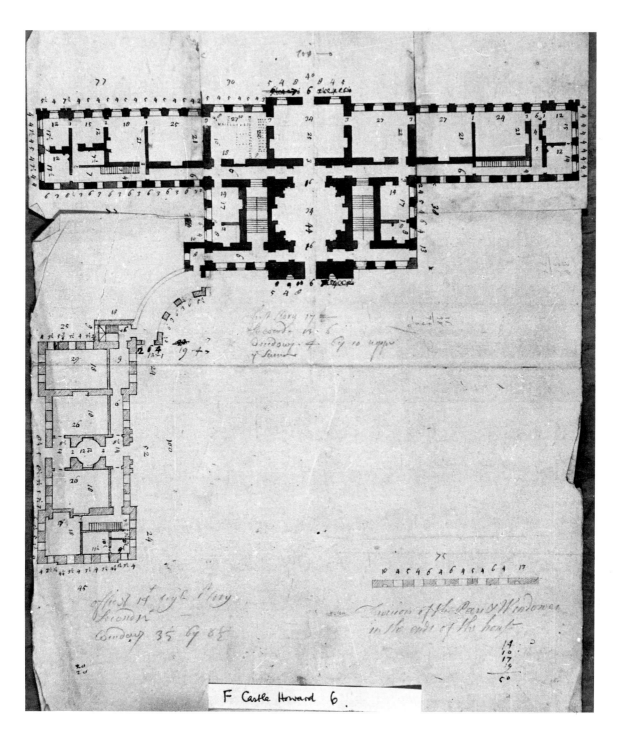

F Castle Howard 6

17. CASTLE HOWARD, Yorkshire. Plan, drawn by Vanbrugh *c* 1699, pen and ink, pencil annotations, on paper (north at the top). *Victoria and Albert Museum, London*, No. E 3296 , 1951 (Photograph: Courtauld Institute of Art). This plan, called by Whistler one of the drawings of the 'Second Proposal', shows how Vanbrugh's emerging ideas first put the kitchen wing (bottom left of illustration) in a block linked to the south front by a corridor running from west to east. The kitchen range was finally incorporated on the east side of the house, and is not visible from the present south garden front (see **10**).

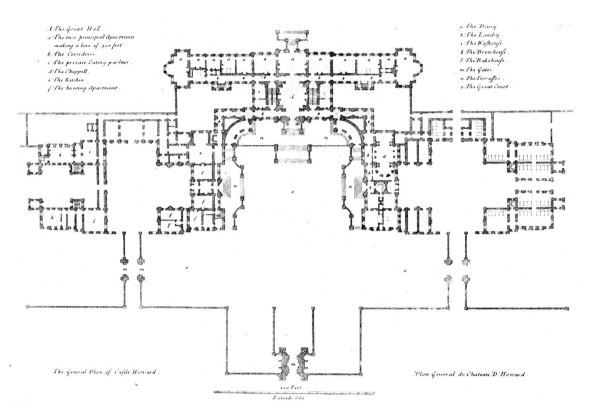

A. The Great Hall
a. The two principall Apartments
   making a line of 300 feet
b. The Corridores
c. The private Eating parlour
d. The Chappell
e. The Kitchin
f. The hunting Apartment

g. The Dairy
h. The Landry
i. The Washhouse
k. The Brewhouse
l. The Bakhouse
m. The Gates
n. The Terrasses
o. The Great Court

The General Plan of Castle Howard.

Plan General du Chateau D'Howard.

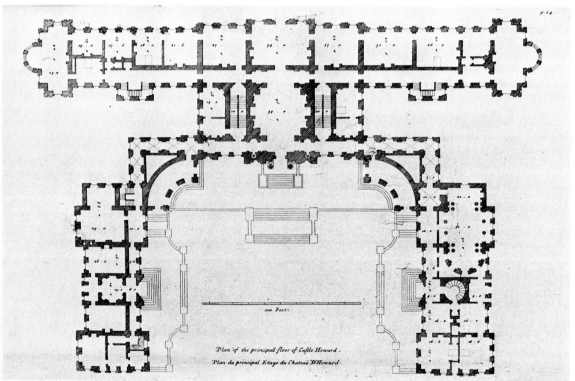

Plan of the principall floor of Castle Howard.

Plan du principal Etage du Chateau D'Howard.

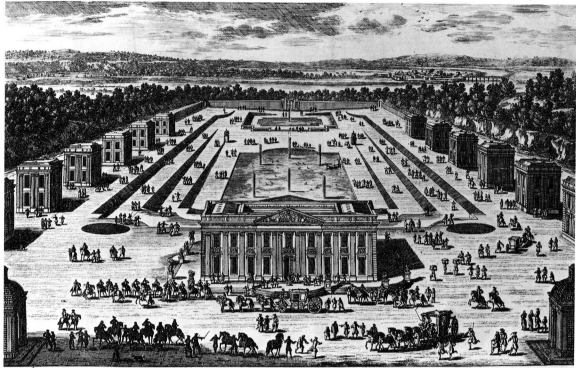

LE CHÂTEAU DE MARLY

A Paris Chez I. Mariette rüe S.ᵗ Iacques à la Victoire · Avec Privilege du Roy.

18-19. CASTLE HOWARD, Yorkshire. The General Plan, and (**19**) the Plan of the Principal Floor, from Colen Campbell, *Vitruvius Britannicus*, I (1715), pls. 63-4 (Photographs: Birmingham Reference Library).

The west wing as shown at the right was built to a design by Sir Thomas Robinson, some twenty-five years after Vanbrugh's death, 1753-9. The Stable Court behind it, originally to balance the Kitchen Court on the east was abandoned. These amendments apart, the Vanbrugh conception – the State Rooms facing south (marked 'a' at top) and the way the Great Hall (A) has been strengthened to take the dome and lantern – can be noted.

20. CHÂTEAU DE MARLY, by Jules Hardouin Mansart (1646-1708). Begun 1679, engraved by Gabriel Pérelle (Photograph: Courtauld Institute of Art).

The importance of French architectural books and engravings to late-seventeenth-century English architects such as Talman and Vanbrugh cannot be under-estimated. Alongside the expected possession of the great Italian works, Alberti, Scamozzi, Serlio, Palladio, the French works may have seemed less vital. However, the 1st Earl of Portland obtained plans of Versailles, the Trianon, and Marly directly from Mansart. The content of Vanbrugh's library is unknown to us, except for his possession of a Paris edition of Palladio (1650) and the translation of the *Quattro Libri* by Leoni (1715). However Wren possessed at least 15 books printed in Paris including Antoine Le Pautre's *Oeuvres d'Architecture* (1652) from which the ideal château drawing (see **45**) may have been used as a source for the Blenheim facades. Certainly the giant pilaster treatment at Blenheim echoes that at Marly, engraved by Pérelle.

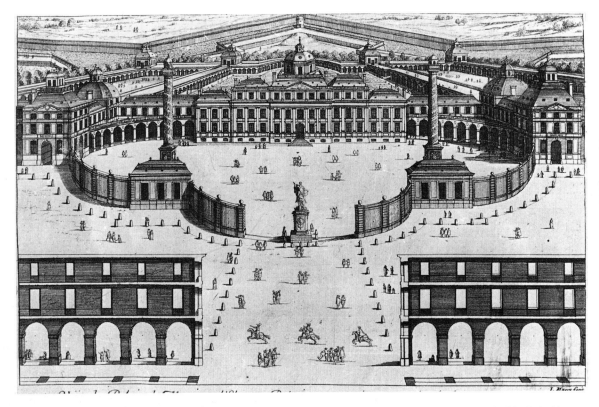

21. MANNHEIM, Germany. The Electoral Palace, engraved by Jean Marot, 1670 (Photograph: Courtauld Institute of Art).

'The final conception, in the relation of the side blocks at Castle Howard to the domed central block, with a longer range of buildings on the garden front, is remarkably close to Jean Marot's design for the palace at Mann-

heim'. Marot's design was published in his *L'Architecture françoise* (Paris *c* 1670) known as the 'Grand Marot'.

This similarity was first established by Professor John Shearman, and should be read in relation to the drawing by Wren of Greenwich Hospital and the engraving of the Collège des Quatre Nations in Paris by Gabriel Pérelle (see **10, 23**).

22. PARIS, Court of the HÔPITAL DES INVALIDES, 1670-7, by Libéral Bruant and Jules Hardouin Mansart (Photograph: Courtauld Institute of Art).

The vast complex of the Invalides was built to house disabled soldiers, with the domed church by Mansart being added later. Designed in the form of a grid the arcaded courts find repetition in varied forms in Vanbrugh's work in England. Taken along with the appearance of Versailles, and the Château de Marly (see **20**) and the possible possession of scores of engravings, as well as architectural works by Jean Marot (see **21**), Le Pautre (see **45**) and Le Muet, 'the character of French architecture, the accomplished use of the classical vocabulary ... and more specifically the French conception of the wall as a variegated rather than a plain surface ...' could have been mastered by any intelligent observer. Wren, from his visit to Paris in 1665 brought back 'almost all France in Paper', and Hawksmoor's wide knowledge of foreign buildings was culled from printed sources.

23. PARIS, COLLÈGE DES QUATRE NATIONS, by Louis Le Vau, begun 1662, engraved by Gabriel Pérelle (Photograph: Courtauld Institute of Art).

In the 1660s Louis Le Vau designed for the executors of Cardinal Mazarin the Collège des Quatre Nations (sometimes called the Collège Mazarin, and now home of the Institut de France). The building on the south side of the Seine, on the axis of the Square Court of the Louvre, has a domed church and quadrants connecting it to wings, not unlike the later north front of Castle Howard (see **8**). We assume that on Vanbrugh's journeyings in France, which of course ceased at his imprisonment there, he may well have seen Le Vau's Collège, and also, as a soldier, been interested in the Hôpital des Invalides (see **22**).

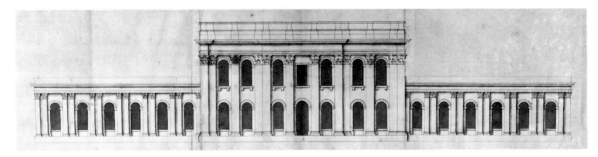

24. CASTLE HOWARD, Yorkshire. 'First Proposal', Elevation of South Front, *c* 1700. Pen, ink and wash on paper, *Victoria and Albert Museum, London*, No. E420, 1951 (Photograph: Museum).

The connecting wings are only of six bays each, whereas the house, as built, has nine. The early ideas show that no consideration was being given to providing a dome, or to the conduct of the facade at its east and west ends. A bow-window, a favourite Vanbrugh feature, was provided at the east end (1706), but that proposed for the west was not built. The windows are round-headed as opposed to the slightly earlier thoughts on the north front, which show rectangular ones (see **13**).

96

25. CASTLE HOWARD, Yorkshire, looking from the south-west, to the Garden Front, 1705–8.

The west wing (at left) which is shown in an earlier proposed form in the view in *Vitruvius Britannicus* was not built within the lifetime of either the 3rd Earl of Carlisle (died 1738) or his architect (died 1726). Indeed the 4th Earl was near the end of his life before he commenced the west wing, *c* 1753, to the designs of his brother-in-law Sir Thomas Robinson (1700–77). The accounts from 1753–9 show that about £4000 was expended on the wing, but heavy gambling debts incurred by the 5th Earl prevented Robinson also replacing Vanbrugh's east wing. Horace Walpole recorded that when Vanbrugh and the youthful Robinson once met at Castle Howard they stood 'spitting and swearing at one another'. The west wing joins the south garden front somewhat awkwardly in an unfortunate over-wide pavilion which unbalances the facade despite having work done on it in the nineteenth century to bring it into some relationship with Vanbrugh's facade.

26-27. CASTLE HOWARD, Yorkshire. Centre of the South Front, with (**27**) a detail of the pediment carvings. The stone 'drapery' on the south front was provided, to that description in his bill, by Samuel Carpenter, and the Huguenot refugee, Nadauld. The '27 Pilaster Capitalls of the Corinthian Order' (of which ten are shown here) were charged at 50s. each. For a further 50s. Carpenter carved 'A Shield and Cherabin head over the window' which we recognize as the keystone of the upper central window. The 'tropheas', tritons and lions on the entablature frieze, were carved by Nadauld, who had a special shed put up on the site for his use. Lord Carlisle's arms were carved within the pediment. Nadauld had carved similar motifs a short time before on the west pediment at Chatsworth.

28. CASTLE HOWARD, Yorkshire. The Satyr Gate, 1705.

Originally the Satyr Gate acted as the principal entrance to the walled garden, which was increased in size after Vanbrugh's death. The stone carver, Samuel Carpenter of York, received £24 for the two stone baskets of flowers, and 30s. for each of four masks: two satyr heads that look outwards, and the two lions' heads (shown here) that look inwards to the gardens. Vanbrugh used lions' heads on a later design for a chimneypiece (*repr.* Whistler, p. 123) but the design for the Satyr Gate is a probable amalgam of the thoughts of Vanbrugh and Hawksmoor, and the abilities of Carpenter.

29. CASTLE HOWARD, Yorkshire. The Kitchen Court from the south, *c* 1710–16.

There is within Vanbrugh's architecture a recurrence of the 'embattled' style, and the four-towered buildings of the East Base Court do give a powerful impression of enclosure to the kitchen court. All the ashlar needed was obtained in the park.

The small pavilions were built 1710–11 with ogee caps derived from the lantern of St Peter's. They were sketched out by Hawksmoor, but the finials had to be replaced with square lanterns to give ventilation, and the 'Large Riseing Ribbs' noted on his drawing were left out.

30. CASTLE HOWARD, Yorkshire. Aerial view of House and Park, looking north (Photograph: Cambridge University, Committee for Aerial Photography).

This view should be compared with the bird's-eye view shown in Colen Campbell's *Vitruvius Britannicus* in 1725 (see **8**). However the Vanbrugh plans for the west wing of the house were not realized, the present buildings on that side being designed by Sir Thomas Robinson, 1753–9. In a map of 1727 the lake is shown as still being dug, and 'when the bridge appears for the first time in the map of 1744 a river has still to be made beneath it.' The Great Lake was in fact not created until 1795–9 'with an embankment built at the north end of the valley which enabled 80 acres to be flooded, forming in fact two lakes linked through a concealed dam'.

31. CASTLE HOWARD, Yorkshire. The Pyramid Gate, 1719.

The outworks at Castle Howard, some done after Vanbrugh's death, are a fascinating study, spreading (as Laurence Whistler has written) 'farther and farther from the house in a widening ripple of fantasy'. The hill-top Pyramid Gate bears the date 1719, and was the first imposing entrance through which visitors from York and London would pass. It frames the obelisk, erected in 1715 by Vanbrugh as Lord Carlisle's tribute to the military victories of the 1st Duke of Marlborough. The wings of the gatehouse were added in 1756 to help with the provision of accommodation for sightseers.

32. CASTLE HOWARD, Yorkshire. North-east corridor from Hall to East Wing.

This corridor is hidden behind the curved arcade or corridor connecting the centre block to the east wing. It acts both as a means of communication and as a 'gallery' for classical sculpture. Within its narrow width, and extreme length 20 metres (65 ft) the stone-masons showed their skills in giving reality to the architect's design of stepped piers, simple vaults, and a long visita tempting one to reach the unknown areas at its end – a Baroque ideal of never-ending fascination, which Vanbrugh and Hawksmoor fully utilized.

33. CASTLE HOWARD, Yorkshire. Interior of the Dome and Lantern, painting destroyed, 1940 (Photograph: National Monuments Record).

From 1709 until receiving their payment in 1712, the Venetian painters Gian Antonio Pellegrini and Marco Ricci worked at Castle Howard. 'The Fall of Phaeton' was painted by Pellegrini on the inner surface of the dome, and the 'Four Elements' on the supporting pendentives. Unfortunately, a fire in November 1940 destroyed the dome and Pellegrini's painting within, as well as ravaging the eastern arm of the south front. The late Lord Howard of Henderskelfe, with great courage, marshalled all the resources, and saw to it that the dome was restored. A pale version of Pelligrini's 'Fall of Phaeton' was repainted in tempera by the Canadian painter, Scott Medd.

The complex iconographic programme at Castle Howard has been examined by Charles Saumarez-Smith, as noted on p. 35. The rooms destroyed by fire were illustrated in 1927 in Tipping and Hussey.

34. CASTLE HOWARD, Yorkshire. The Hall from the East Staircase, 1706-10.

Vanbrugh's involvement with the Italian stuccoists and painters occurred in one or other of their skills at Castle Howard, Blenheim, Kimbolton and Seaton Delaval, as well as paintings occurring at King's Weston and Grimsthorpe. Here *scagliola* (or artificial stone paste simulating marble) is used to create a niche to face the stucco overmantel. The pendentives, and dome overhead (see **33**) were painted by Pellegrini, helped by Marco Ricci.

35. BLENHEIM PALACE, Oxfordshire. The East Gate, 1708, amended 1773–5.

By November 1708 the East Gate was 4 metres (14 ft) high. Vanbrugh designed it so that it could incorporate a cistern over the arch leading to the eastern kitchen court. To this water was pumped by Aldersea's Engine. In 1773 Neo-Classical embellishments (rope-like swags, fruit branch motif in the upper side panels, lions' heads, possibly the iron gates) were added by Sir William Chambers. In 1775 the 4th Duke, who wanted to soften the 'rude' aspect of Vanbrugh's design, added the two statues in the niches from a group removed from the top of the north court.

The legend over the keystone reads:

UNDER THE AUSPICES OF A MUNIFICENT SOVEREIGN THIS HOUSE WAS BUILT FOR JOHN, DUKE OF MARLBOROUGH, AND HIS DUCHESS SARAH, BY SIR J. VANBRUGH BETWEEN THE YEARS 1709 AND 1722, AND THIS ROYAL MANOR OF WOODSTOCK, TOGETHER WITH A GRANT OF £240,000 TOWARDS THE BUILDING OF BLENHEIM WAS GIVEN BY HER MAJESTY QUEEN ANNE AND CONFIRMED BY ACT OF PARLIAMENT (3 & 4 ANNE, C.4) TO THE SAID JOHN, DUKE OF MARLBOROUGH AND TO ALL HIS ISSUE MALE AND FEMALE LINEALLY DESCENDING.

36. THE 1st DUKE and DUCHESS OF MARLBOROUGH.
Painting, by Enoch Seeman (1694–1745), oil on canvas,
The Lord Montagu of Beaulieu.

Enoch Seeman was a native of Dantzig who came to
London about 1715 and soon found good employment.
His double portrait, with life-size figures of John Churchill and Sarah Jennings (later the 1st Duke and Duchess) is partly after Kneller's style, in that both are
depicted in their late thirties. The couple had married in
1678 when John Churchill was 28, and Sarah 18. Comparison can be made with Closterman's portrait of the
Duke and Kneller's head and shoulders oval portrait of
the Duchess at Althrop.

37. SIR GODFREY KNELLER. Allegorical Sketch, 1708,
for an intended painting of Queen Anne presenting an
elevation of Blenheim to 'Military Merit'. *The Duke of
Marlborough.*

Kneller described his allegorical painting as being intended for the upper end of the Long Gallery at Blenheim. He was to represent the Queen as the figure of
Generosity giving to a figure representing Military Merit
a model of Blenheim drawn on paper. Victory is next to
Hercules at the left, and figures of Plenty and History to
the right. Apollo is at the centre top commanding Fame
to proclaim and signify the same 'to the whole Universe'.

The sketch passed through the collections of Dr Mead,
the Duchess of Newcastle, and Lord Pelham who gave it
to the Duke of Marlborough in 1800. The painting was
'not performed in Large' due to the differences between
the Queen and the 1st Duke.

38. WOODSTOCK MANOR, Oxfordshire. Engraving, 1714, *British Library*, Map Room K, XXXV, 28.d. (Photograph: Library).

The historian Thomas Hearne attested that Woodstock Manor was 'first built by King Henry I, who made the Park, and afterwards augmented by Henry II ...'. To Henry I and Henry II Woodstock was a hunting lodge. Later monarchs enlarged the house, particularly Henry VII. Enough of it survived by the early eighteenth century for views to be engraved, and for Vanbrugh, a devoted advocate of the medieval style, to patch it up, and live there, on and off, for three years. He defended the retention of the ruins, but the determination of the Duchess 'effected what Cromwell's cannon had failed to do; to leave no stone standing upon another, and to remove even the foundations, to make a causeway.'

39. BLENHEIM PALACE, Oxfordshire. 'Plan of Woodstock Park with Blenheim House, Gardens &c', engraved in Colen Campbell, *Vitruvius Britannicus*, III (1725) pls. 71-2 (Photograph: Birmingham Reference Library).

Compared with the original layout for Blenheim gardens and park by Henry Wise and John Vanbrugh (see **42**) this engraved view marks the Bridge (H) (see **67**) on its axial alignment with the north front of the house (see **46**).

40. BLENHEIM PALACE, Oxfordshire. General Plan, Colen Campbell, *Vitruvius Britannicus*, I (1715) pl. 62 (Photograph: Birmingham Reference Library).

Whilst the main block and the east and west wings were modelled on Castle Howard (see **18**) some improvements were made, with the office courts being added to the scheme, *c* 1707. The plan enables the scale of the forecourt, and the way the wings project to its east and west, to be appreciated.

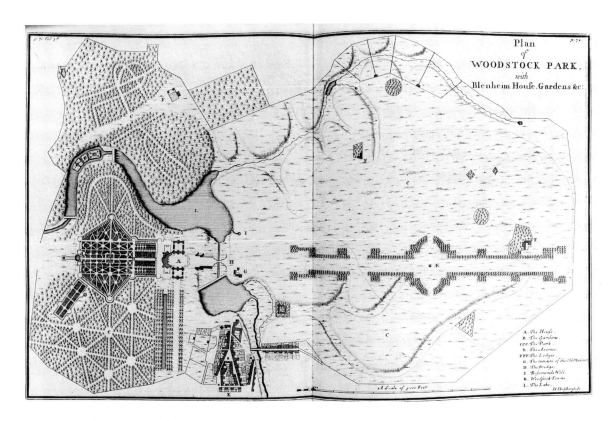

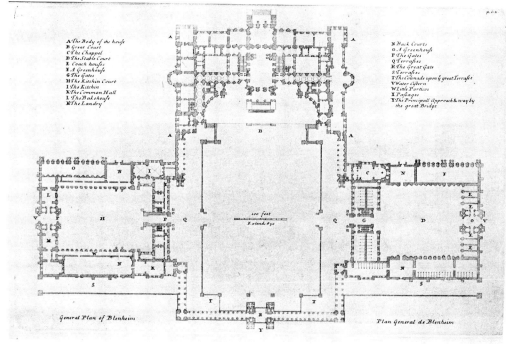

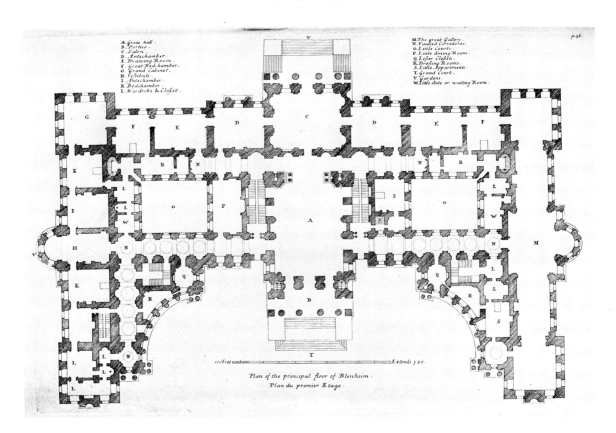

Plan of the principal floor of Blenheim.
Plan du premier Etage.

41. BLENHEIM PALACE, Oxfordshire, Plan of the Principal Floor, or *piano nobile*, Colen Campbell, *Vitruvius Britannicus*, I (1715) pls. 65-6 (Photograph: Birmingham Reference Library).

The plan graphically illustrates the relationship between the central block, the Great Hall (A) and Saloon (C), and the quadrant colonnades and rooms leading to the east wing (G to L) and west wing (M). The Duchess of Marlborough's favourite bow window room was in the east wing (H) and the Great Gallery (now Long Library) occupied the whole length of the west front (M).

42. BLENHEIM PALACE, Oxfordshire. 'A Plann of Blenheim' – the Gardens and Park by Henry Wise and John Vanbrugh, 1709. Pen, ink and coloured wash, on paper, s. & d. '1709 Bridgeman Descript', 129.5 × 70.2 cm (52 × 28 ins) *His Grace The Duke of Marlborough*.

This plan was drawn out by Charles Bridgeman, who helped Henry Wise from time to time, after Wise's partner, George London, had died. Years later Bridgeman was to succeed Wise as Royal Gardner to George II. This drawing is similar to the plan of 1725 shown in *Vitruvius Britannicus*, III (1725) (see **39**). 'The scheme is dominated by the great avenue of beeches which still remains, and by the road across the Great Bridge' (see **67**) on its way to the north front. An aerial view (see **43**) reinforces the majestic lines of the original layout, which may owe as much to Bridgeman, who signs the plan, as to Vanbrugh and Wise.

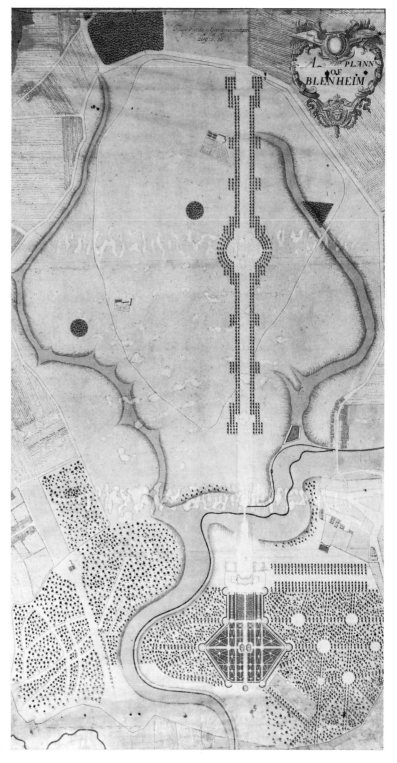

43. BLENHEIM PALACE, Oxfordshire. Aerial view of House and Park, looking north (Photograph: Cambridge University, Committee for Aerial Photography).

This view should be compared with Vanbrugh and Henry Wise's original layout for gardens and park (see **42**). Much of the formality was swept away by Capability Brown, but the axial alignment of trees stretching out to the Column of Victory (designed by Henry Herbert, Lord Pembroke, and erected 1727–31) is an impressive survival. The Great Avenue was replanted in 1902 with the central motif changed from an ellipse to a square. The length of the avenue is 2255 metres (7400 ft).

44. CHÂTEAU DE VAUX-LE-VICOMTE. Entrance Front, 1657–61, engraving by Nicolas de Poilly (Photograph: Courtauld Institute of Art).

When Vanbrugh was confined to the Château of Vincennes during his imprisonment in France he would have had Louis Le Vau's work around him. The French architect had built Vincennes at the command of Cardinal Mazarin. Vanbrugh may have also been able to see his Collège Mazarin in Paris (see **23**), and probably the great complex of Vaux-le-Vicomte which Le Vau had built for Nicolas Fouquet, 1657–61. The grouping on the entrance side with its two flanking base-courts may have been the exemplar for the disposition of the elements on the north front at Blenheim (see **46**). Stylistic influence-spotting is however a pastime which can mislead. What is important is that the buildings concerned may have led Vanbrugh towards a keen appreciation of architecture, and to eclectic borrowing from these or similar prototypes in later years.

45. ANTOINE LE PAUTRE (1621–81). Design for a château, engraving in his *Oeuvres d'Architecture*, (1652), pl. 27 (Photograph: Birmingham Reference Library).

This great château, of bold plan and elevation, was one of those designs for country and town houses which Le Pautre had not been able to execute. In the engravings 'unrestrained by the ties of practical considerations … Le Pautre gives free rein to his imagination, and creates a series of designs which have hardly any parallel in French architecture.' Here the colossal order, the concave pavilions which link the end pavilions, the rusticated surfaces, the drum and domes were motifs to be studied by the theatrically minded such as Vanbrugh. Similarities may be found in his facades at Blenheim.

46. BLENHEIM PALACE, Oxfordshire. The North Front, 1705–1716.

The main pile of Blenheim, owing something in conception to prototypes such as the château of Vaux-le-Vicomte (1657–61, see **44**) was entrusted to the masons Edward Strong and his son to erect. They worked hard in 1705–6 and the central block was up to the principal floor by May 1706. By November 1708 the imposing Portico (see **48**) was over 8 metres (28ft) high, and at the end of the winter Henry Wise was levelling the Great Court and forming the north-west approach. The need for funds and for more Cornbury stone was urgent and the Duke forbade any work on the kitchen court until the main pile was completed. All were at work on a palace, the Nation's gift, and despite its troublous building history, the mass finally extended to 260 metres (850

ft) with the north front of a length of 145 metres (480 ft). The two wings (see **40**) stretched northward from the central block some 70 metres (225 ft). The Great Court covering an area of three acres, was aligned on the Great Avenue and bridge (see **43**).

In the tympanum of the north portico (see **47**), Grinling Gibbons carved the Duke's arms. The statuary now surviving on the balustrade level with the pediment, and shown in *Vitrivius Britannicus* (I, 1715, pls 57, 58) was replaced by the 9th Duke of Marlborough in 1804, with terracotta statues from France. No bill has ever been found for those shown in Campbell's *Vitruvius Britannicus* but Gibbons had carved 13 (of an intended 18) statues for the north front and its quadrants. Two survive in the niches on the east gate (see **35**).

47. BLENHEIM PALACE, Oxfordshire. The East Colonnade, and Entrance to the kitchen court, 1706–8.

By October 1707, a little over two years from the laying of the foundation stone (18 June 1705) Matthew Banckes had finished the masonry work of the east colonnade. Work had been pushed along hard on the kitchen court (with attention focussed on the clock tower, which John Townesend finished in August 1708. There was also much activity in carving by Grinling Gibbons's team on the stone finials and trophies – especially three lions mauling the French cockerels.

48. BLENHEIM PALACE, Oxfordshire. The North Front, detail of the Entrance Portico.

For a note on the north front see that to **46**. For the trophy carvings at the foot of the stairs, see **52.**

49. BLENHEIM PALACE, Oxfordshire. The clock tower, kitchen court, 1707–8.

The visitor approaching Blenheim now passes through the east gate (see **35**), then through the kitchen court, with John Townesend's clock tower, before passing through another imposing entrance in the east wing to enter the Great Court before the north front.

John Townesend (1648–1728) was head of a prominent family of Oxford masons. Both John, and his son William (d. 1739) worked at Blenheim, the latter in partnership with Bartholomew Peisley III (c 1683–1727).

50. BLENHEIM PALACE, Oxfordshire. The colonnade of the east kitchen court, 1706–7.

The early years in Blenheim's long building history were naturally given over to the extensive activity of the team of masons. Whilst the Strongs concentrated on the main pile and the east wing, Henry Banckes was at work on the colonnades, chapel, kitchen and the middle frontis-piece of the south front (see **56**). The position of the kitchen court colonnade (shown here in detail) may be seen in **40**. Here are some of the favourite Vanbrugh motifs – heavy key-stones, round-headed arches and dominant entrances.

51. BLENHEIM PALACE, Oxfordshire. Detail of the East Wing lantern and finials carved by Grinling Gibbons and his assistants, 1708–12.

Gibbons and his assistants dealt with the enrichment of thousands of yards of masonry but the coronetted finials on the four great towers (1709) are the most impressive. They were charged as 'carv'd Pinacles, the Scrolls a flower De Luce revers'd and Corronett upon the Same, in all 30 ft high, at £20 each.'

52. BLENHEIM PALACE, Oxfordshire. Stone trophy by Grinling Gibbons, plinth, west side of steps, north portico, c 1710.

Grinling Gibbon's first bill for work at Blenheim is dated September 1708. With his team of craftsmen he did much work in stone and marble (but, surprisingly, at Blenheim did little carved woodwork). Whilst the helm on this trophy has slumped from a higher position (see the 1927 illustrations in Tipping and Hussey) the emphasis is still evident: the accoutrements of military activity interpreted in a Roman manner. The range of work from ground level to roof level is impressive, even allowing for the fact that much has been lost.

53-54. BLENHEIM PALACE, Oxfordshire. Vanbrugh's south front in the Doric Order, *Bodleian Library, Oxford*, MS., Top. Oxon., a.37*, folio 8 (Photograph: Library), and (**54**) as executed (except for the statuary and trophies), Colen Campbell, *Vitruvius Britannicus*, I (1715) pls. 59-60 (Photograph: Birmingham Reference Library).

Whilst Vanbrugh contended that he had not deviated from the original wooden model approved by the Queen, in 1707 the Strongs had to pull down 'the two sixty-foot stretches on ye south front joining to ye south-east and south-west pavilions, the former being 27 feet high ... the latter 13 ft ... Also pulling down the $37\frac{1}{2}$ ft stretches on the east side the south portico.' This drastic amendment was to change the architectural order from Doric to Corinthian. The whole silhouette was altered, incorporating eventually the addition of the impressive corner lanterns, and an overall increase in height of nearly one third.

Vanbrugh, tossing the idea about with Hawksmoor and his craftsmen, rarely made a bolder move in amending an already impressive façade.

55-56. BLENHEIM PALACE, Oxfordshire. The South Front, and a detail of the centre.

The centre of the south front breaks forward into an applied portico of three bays flanked by square-cut columns with fine Corinthian capitals. Set atop is the great bust of Louis XIV which the Duke of Marlborough took from the Porte Royale of the Citadel in Tournai, a town he captured in 1709. The bust weighing some four or five tons reached London in April 1712 and was set up soon after. The inscription on the entablature beneath, in Latin, translates as, 'The assertor of the liberty of Europe dedicates these lofty honours to the genius of Britain.'

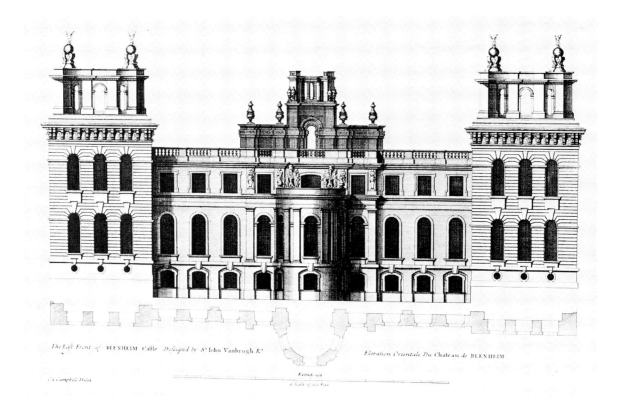

The East Front of BLENHEIM Castle Designd by Sʳ John Vanbrugh Kᵗ

Elevation Orientale Du Chateau de BLENHEIM

C. Campbell Delin

57. BLENHEIM PALACE, Oxfordshire. Elevation of the East Front, Colen Campbell, *Vitruvius Britannicus*, I (1715) pl. 61 (Photograph: Birmingham Reference Library).

The original design for the east front had the same caps to the corner pavilions as those proposed on the elevation of the south front (see **53**). The box-window was a favourite, both with Vanbrugh (he used it on several occasions – listed as seventeen by Whistler, p. 47) and with the Duchess of Marlborough. The elevation in *Vitruvius Britannicus* is more or less as executed, the imposing central feature being the chimney tower (for this front see **58**).

58. BLENHEIM PALACE, Oxfordshire. The East Front, 1705–8.

Reference to the General Plan (see **40**) under the letters A, I, N, will make the position of the east wing in relation to the kitchen area apparent. The counterpoise of the dominant lanterns, pedimented kitchen area and clock tower is one of the impressive features about the Blenheim skyline. The formal gardens were restored by Achille Duchêne in 1925–8 for the 9th Duke of Marlborough.

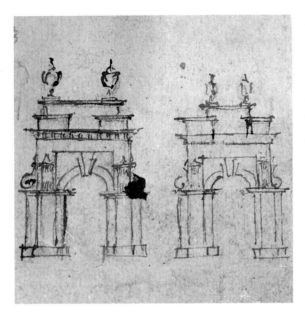

59. BLENHEIM PALACE, Oxfordshire Sketch for Gateways, *c* 1706 (?), pen and ink on paper, William Proby, Esq. (Photograph: Courtauld Institute of Art).

This drawing of two keystone gateways is in the style of the East Gate at Blenheim. However it would be wrong to connect what are merely attractive pencillings, to an important feature of the house, when further evidence, such as an inscription, or intent, is lacking.

60. BLENHEIM PALACE, Oxfordshire. Project (unexecuted) possibly by Sir James Thornhill, for the western wall of the Great Hall, pen, ink and wash on paper, 1706, *His Grace, The Duke of Marlborough.*

This spirited scheme seems to have been based on an arrangement in the seventeenth century of actual weapons, first in the Tower of London, and then in the Guard Chamber at Hampton Court. The late Edward Croft-Murray, the authority on decorative painting in England, suggested that while the trophies were clearly three-dimensional, the weapons on the wall were probably to be painted. Thornhill's schemes for Hall and Saloon would probably have enlivened the severe architecture; that he did so little (see **62**) due to the concerns with economy is a matter for regret.

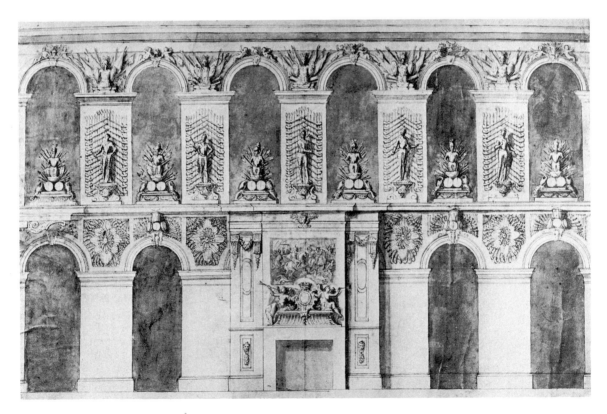

61. BLENHEIM PALACE, Oxfordshire. Design for the Saloon, pen, ink and wash on paper, *Bodleian Library, Oxford*, MS., Top. Oxon., a.37* folio 32 (Photograph: Library).

The first idea for the Saloon which Vanbrugh and Hawksmoor proposed consisted again of round-headed recesses between Corinthian pilasters, a further echo of the Great Hall. However a French artist, Louis Silvestre, prepared a long critique of it in September 1707, and sent his own scheme. He was seemingly no threat, however, to the established team, and the scheme with niches and giant statues remained the accepted one until work was resumed in 1716, after the long period of inactivity when the money ran out.

Re-examination after Vanbrugh had been dismissed caused a radical change. The niches, which Grinling Gibbons had already carved (for the ten-foot stautes Vanbrugh was trying to acquire from Italy) were to disappear beneath the paintings of Louis Laguerre.

62. BLENHEIM PALACE, Oxfordshire. Ceiling of the Great Hall. Painted, oil on plaster, 1716.

Whilst James Thornhill (he was not knighted until 1720), painter of the ceiling in the Great Hall, had a considerable reputation, based on his Greenwich (Painted Hall) and St Paul's Cathedral ceilings, he was held in as much disfavour as Vanbrugh by Sarah, Duchess of Marlborough. She thought that 'though painters had very high flights, they must be kept down'. The Hall was ready for painting by the autumn of 1711, and some remarkable schemes were proposed for it, and for the Saloon (see **61**). However, work ceased until 1716 when the Duke set about finishing Blenheim at his own expense, but suffering two strokes he relinquished control of the works to his wife, a rich but very mean woman. For the grand historical part of the ceiling, the 'Glorification of the Duke of Marlborough', Thornhill wanted to charge 25s a yard. The other ornament on the walls was left to an assistant, but there was to be no abatement in the rate charged. The bill amounted to £575 5s. for the ceiling, and £402 15s. for the attic walls, a total of £978. Vanbrugh endorsed it as correct, and whilst Thornhill was paid this amount his charges led to the commission for the Saloon being given to Louis Laguerre.

63. BLENHEIM PALACE, Oxfordshire. Marble statue of Queen Anne, by J. M. Rysbrack, finished 1738.

On 26 June 1735 Sarah, Duchess of Marlborough wrote to her grand-daughter Lady Diana Spencer 'I am going to Rysbrack to make a bargain with him for a fine statue of Queen Anne, which I will put up in the bow window room at Blenheim with a proper inscription. It will be a very fine thing and though but one figure will cost me £300. I have a satisfaction in showing this respect to her, because her kindness to me was real. And what happened afterwards was compassed by the contrivance of such as are in power now.'

It was finally installed in October 1738 in the western bow in the Gallery (not the bow-window room in the east wing). It was moved, at the installation of the Father Willis organ, to its present position at the north end of the Long Library. The inscription on the pedestal reads:

To

The Memory

of

QUEEN ANN

under whose Auspices

JOHN DUKE OF MARLBOROUGH

Conquered

And to whose Munificence

He and His Posterity

with Gratitude

Owe the Possession

of

BLENHEIM

A:D: MDCCXXXX:VI:

64. BLENHEIM PALACE. Oxfordshire. The Great Hall, 1706-10; 1716.

When work at Blenheim was halted in October 1710 the whole palace, except for the West Towers, was roofed. By 1710 Edward Strong and his men had also fluted the shafts of the engaged columns and pilasters, whilst Grinling Gibbons and his team had enriched the capitals above with furling acanthus, and carved the great cornice.

In arrangement, the arcaded side walls, perhaps too massive – and in a Hall which, as at Castle Howard, was too high – serve to light two staircases (of which only one survives on the east side). An upper corridor is carried across the end, supported by great console brackets by Gibbons 'cutt extrordinary rich and sunk very deep'. The elliptical arch at the end leads through to the Saloon. The 'nothing done' plan of the principal floor prepared in 1716 by Tilleman Bobart, the Blenheim Comptroller, showed the Great Hall, marked: 'Painting & Upper Windows and Paveing to do'. In this year (1716), Thornhill was allowed to resume his painting of the ceiling (**62**) and upper walls, and had finished them by December. Would that he could have carried out his first proposed scheme (**60**). However, his high charges earned the displeasure of the Duchess, who gave the commission for painting in the Saloon to Louis Laguerre.

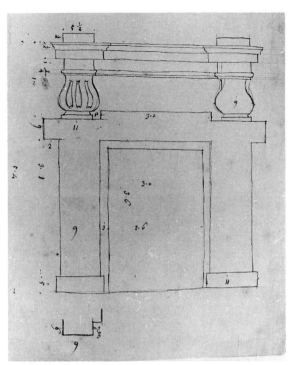

65. BLENHEIM PALACE, Oxfordshire. Drawing for a fireplace (?), ink on paper, *William Proby Esq.* (Photograph: Courtauld Institute of Art).
The drawing has a resemblance to the marble chimney-piece in the Duchess of Marlborough's Bedchamber, provided by Grinling Gibbons, but dating from after Vanbrugh had ceased to be involved with the great problems attendant on the building.

66. BLENHEIM PALACE, Oxfordshire. Engraving of Vanbrugh's bridge by H. Terasson, 1739, *Society of Antiquaries* (Photograph: Courtauld Institute of Art).
The bridge, begun in July 1708, can no longer be seen as Terasson saw it, due to the alteration in water level caused by Capability Brown's landscaping (see **43**). The arcaded superstructure was not however built. There are three different engravings of the bridge, which vary in the foreign inscriptions; there are four inscriptions in this case, Latin, English, French and Dutch.

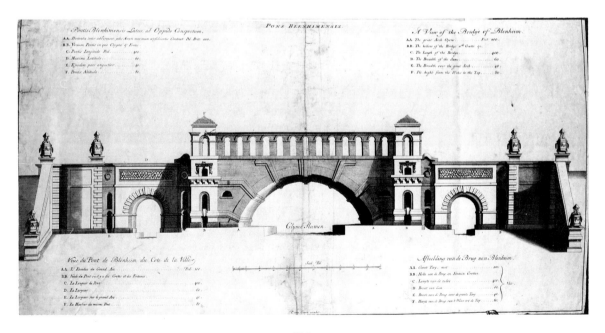

67. BLENHEIM PALACE, Oxfordshire. The west side of the Grand Bridge, 1708-21.

The main section of Vanbrugh's Grand Bridge was founded in July 1708, but severe weather that winter caused repairs to be made to it in April 1709. By September Bartholomew Peisley, Snr., its mason-builder, had keyed the main arch. Vanbrugh also seems to have had incorporated three medieval stones from Woodstock Manor. Then work halted until February 1712 when Peisley started work on the bridge again. Henry Wise's teams were at work on the causeways in June 1716, but again all activity ceased when the final rift between Sarah, Duchess and Vanbrugh occurred. It was not until 1721 that William Townesend and Bartholomew Peisley, Jnr., as partners, finished the bridge, and in 1722 made the canals which gave it a proper expanse of water to span. The northernmost arch housed Aldersea's engine which raised water to the east cistern tower (see **35**).

The arcading shown in Terasson's engraving (see **66**) the Duchess refused Vanbrugh permission to add. The massive effect was further diminished in 1764 when Capability Brown enlarged the lake, by building a dam above Bladon, and releasing in a daring move, the waters of the River Glyme, allowing them to course through the many rooms of the bridge, and find their own level in the surrounding parkland.

The Elevation of a New Design for a person of Quality in Dorsetshire as Designed by Sr John Vanbrugh Kt.
Elevation D'un Nouveau Dessein.

Co. Campbell Delin.   H Hulsbergh Sc.

68. EASTBURY, Dorset. Sketch by Vanbrugh for the Entrance Front, c 1713 (?) pen, ink and wash on paper, *Victoria & Albert Museum, London*, Nos. D129-91 (Photograph: Courtauld Institute of Art).
This is probably the first of many sketched ideas for the development of Eastbury, which needed several highly finished drawings as it proceeded. Most architects had draughtsmen within their offices who worked up first sketches into scale drawings. The drawing gives a good idea of Vanbrugh's powerful realization of a facade, with a double Palladian, or Venetian, emphasis in the door and window openings of the centre bay.

69. EASTBURY, Dorset. Elevation of Garden Front, c 1716, pen, ink and wash, *Victoria and Albert Museum, London*, No. D114-91 (Photograph: Museum).
Vanbrugh first sketched the entrance front (see **68**) and then worked up two more finished drawings, one for the 'Fore Front', and, here illustrated, for the 'Garden Front'. The design does not yet have pavilions to left and right. The attractive bow rising through two storeys was a favourite Vanbrugh feature, deriving from the one at Blenheim, and is here flanked by Corinthian pilasters, which span the width of the Saloon.

70. EASTBURY, Dorset. Elevation of 'a New Design for a person of Quality in Dorsetshire ...', Colen Campbell, *Vitruvius Britannicus*, II (1717) pl. 53 (Photograph: Birmingham Reference Library).
According to Campbell, the 'New Design' was made in 1716 for 'a person of Quality', that is George Dodington, who had bought the property in 1709. The entrance front still retains the open arcaded chimneystacks shown in the earlier elevations of c 1713 (see **68-69**). The garden front with its handsome bow was given a perron staircase. The side of the design acquired the coupled columns and Venetian windows which were shown as part of the earlier entrance front (see **68**).

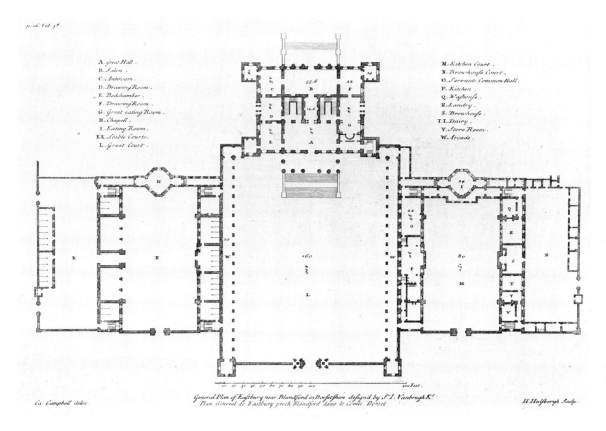

A. Great Hall.
B. Salon.
C. Antiroom.
D. Drawing Room.
E. Bedchamber.
F. Drawing Room.
G. Great eating Room.
H. Chapell.
I. Eating Room.
KK. Stable Courts.
L. Great Court.

M. Kitchen Court.
N. Brew-house Court.
O. Servants Common Hall.
P. Kitchen.
Q. Wash-house.
R. Landry.
S. Brew-house.
T.T. Dairy.
V. Store Room.
W. Arcade.

Ca. Campbell delin

General Plan of Eastbury near Blandford in Dorsetshire design'd by Sʳ I. Vanbrugh Kᵗ.
Plan General de Eastbury proch Blandford dans le Comte Dorset

H. Hulsbergh Sculp.

71. EASTBURY, Dorset. General Plan, *c* 1721, Colen Campbell, *Vitruvius Britannicus*, III (1725) pl. 16 (Photograph: Birmingham Reference Library).
'Eastbury was shortlived and prodigious and its end was melodramatic'. Certainly the design is one to which many amendments and second thoughts were given. It was therefore a somewhat tardy building progress, and the house was not completed until twelve years after Vanbrugh's death. The final plan, a year or two later than Campbell dates it (1718), shows a rectangular form to the Saloon (B on plan) where there was previously a bow-window room. The staircases are also turned to face the Great Hall (A on plan). Today only part of the stable wing, (K on plan), and a great gateway to the north court survive (see **78-79**).

72-73. EASTBURY, Dorset. Elevation of 'One End of a New Design for a person of Quality in Dorsetshire', Colen Campbell, *Vitruvius Britannicus*, II 1717 pl. 55 (Photograph: Birmingham Reference Library) and (**73**) Elevation of the Entrance Front, *Victoria and Albert Museum, London*, No. D118-91 (Photograph: Museum). In the early elevations for Eastbury Vanbrugh developed his ideas, firstly with two chimneys in a single arcade, repeated either side of the central block (see **68-70**). This was still the order by the time Campbell was issuing the second volume of *Vitruvius Britannicus* (1717). The arcaded form with Venetian windows can be seen in its bold form in the elevation of one end of the 'New Design' which perhaps derived from the earlier elevation for the garden front (see **69**). The change from the Corinthian to the Doric Order came next; the towers were raised and the chimneys put in a five-bay arcade at the centre as at King's Weston (see **87**). The final stage can be seen as rusticated and dominant (see **74**).

128

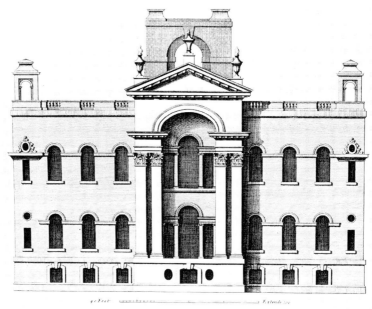

The Elevation of One End of a New Design for a person of Quality in Dorsetshire, as Designed by Sr. John Vanbrugh Kt.

Ca. Campbell Delin.

H. Hulsbergh Sc.

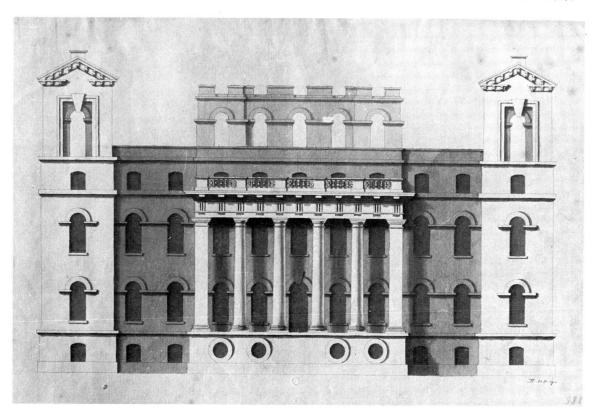

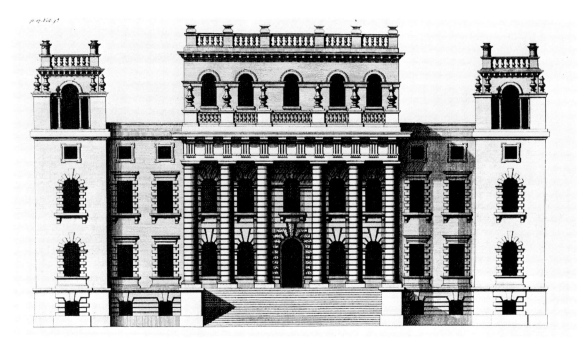

74. EASTBURY, Dorset. Final design, Entrance Front, *c* 1721, Colen Campbell, *Vitruvious Britannicus*, III (1725) pl. 17 (Photograph: Birmingham Reference Library).

The long gestation towards the final appearance of Eastbury is represented in a group of drawings published by Campbell. The chimneys are set in a handsome arcade, but the arches now contain windows which light the stairs (see 'A' on General Plan, **71**). This feature was not however built by Roger Morris (who proceeded with the building after Vanbrugh's death). He also gave the portico a pediment (see **76**). Morris was also involved with the design of Dodington's London house.

75. EASTBURY, Dorset. 'Plan and Elevation of the Bagnio in the Garden ...', 1718, Colen Campbell, *Vitruvius Britannicus*, III (1725) pl. 19 (Photograph: Birmingham Reference Library).

The Bagnio, one of the two garden buildings designed for Eastbury. It was dwarfed by the Temple, a massive structure almost as high as the portico of Gibb's St Martin-in-the-Fields, and worthy of the creator of the Blenheim bridge (see **66**). The Bagnio was erected, as a water-pavilion, half-way along the right edge of Charles Bridgeman's garden layout. Nothing now remains of both buildings, although traces of the garden layout itself survived to recent years.

76-79. EASTBURY, Dorset. The surviving North Wing (**78**) the gateway to the North Court, and (**76-77**) two paintings, oil on canvas, of the entrance and garden fronts in the 1760s.

The total cost of the house and gardens at Eastbury was some £140,000, but it was still unfinished at Vanbrugh's death. George Bubb Dodington, nephew of the first builder, employed Roger Morris to carry on the work. He completed it in 1738 but without the clerestory and with a pediment over the portico. Dodington died in 1762 (as Baron Melcombe) and Lord Temple who

acquired Eastbury only lived there a further thirteen years. In 1775 he demolished the main house, and today only part of the stable wing, and the archway to the north court remain. Its appearance after Morris's work may be judged in two paintings at the house. The main building and everything to the right of it was later demolished. The left forecourt wing and the arch survive, as shown. The companion painting of the garden front shows the portico, and the two octagon rooms, 'H' and 'J' on the General Plan (see **71**), but without the pyramidal roofs shown in Morris's drawing of 1733.

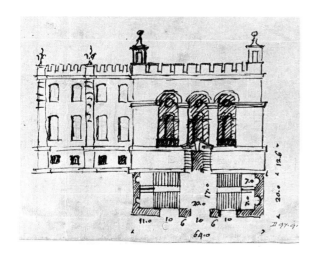

80. KIMBOLTON CASTLE, Cambridgeshire. Design for east entrance, *c* 1707, pen and ink on paper, *Victoria and Albert Museum*, *London*, No. D97. 91 (Photograph: Museum).

This sketch, probably done by Vanbrugh, seems to represent 'an abandoned idea for the east portico'. For the building history of Kimbolton, for one of Vanbrugh's early patrons (the Earl, later 1st Duke of Manchester). See pp. 51-3.

81. KIMBOLTON CASTLE, Cambridgeshire. The East and South Front, 1708-19.

On the east front the Doric portico was added by the Florentine architect, Alessandro Galilei in 1719. He had spent five years in England, 1714-19 in the hope of getting commissions. It is perhaps somewhat unsympathetic to Vanbrugh's facades, although his work at Kimbolton was determined somewhat by the disposition of the earlier house.

82. AUDLEY END, Essex. Stone screen, south end of Great Hall, 1708, and (121) from the staircase side.

On 27 July 1708 Vanbrugh wrote to the Earl of Manchester 'My Ld. Bindon is busy to the utmost of his Force in New Moulding Audley End.' As a distant relative (he became 6th Earl of Suffolk in 1709) Lord Bindon used Vanbrugh's services, and the north and south sides of the outer court and the great kitchen were demolished ready for new works.

Whilst the stone screen and staircase beyond have been traditionally attributed to Vanbrugh, the upper stage was reconstructed in 1763–4. Careful research by Paul Drury leads to his summary:

> It is thus possible – no more – that the lower part of the screen is by Vanbrugh, and the staircase, ground floor arch, and stone doorcase to the saloon were added *c* 1725, either because the original scheme had not been completed, or to replace a (perhaps steeper) staircase of *c* 1708.

83. CHARGATE, Surrey. Sketch Plan and Elevation, ink on paper, William Proby Esq.
The elevation is shown in a stronger worked-up form in **84**. The H-plan measurements indicate that the rooms in the wings were small, with an overall facade of little more than 30 m (100 ft). A similar sketch is in the Victoria & Albert Museum, No. 94.91.

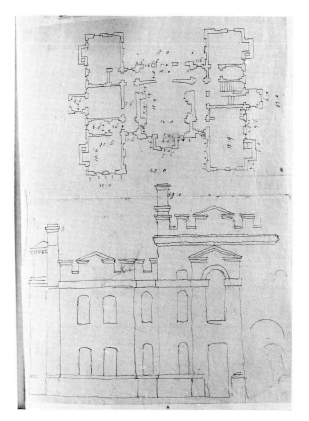

84. CHARGATE, Surrey. Drawing by Vanbrugh, *c* 1703, pen, ink and wash on paper, *Victoria & Albert Museum, London*, No. D124-91 (Photograph: Courtauld Institute of Art).
This was Vanbrugh's own house at Esher, but rarely used. In October 1714 he sold the property to the Earl of Clare (later 1st Duke of Newcastle) who renamed it Claremont, and used Vanbrugh to enlarge it. The battlements were removed, and the small house became the centre block of an extensive pile, shown in an engraving by John Rocque in 1738. The house was demolished in 1769 to make way for the present house, designed by Capability Brown, 1771-4. Vanbrugh's Belvedere still survives (see **86**).

85. CLAREMONT, Surrey. The Belvedere, 1715.
In 1714 the Duke of Newcastle bought Chargate from Vanbrugh (see **83–84**) and renamed it Claremont. Vanbrugh's Belvedere, a small summer retreat, is set on a small hill behind the later house, and is built of brick, with two square battlemented towers on each side. It is an effective summation of Vanbrugh's concern with medieval forms, despite having been vandalized in recent years. The National Trust has cleared a view to it, and put back a semblance of glazing bars when boarding the door and window openings.

86. NEWCASTLE PEW, Esher Old Church, Surrey, 1723–5 (Photograph: National Monuments Record).
On 6 August 1724 a faculty was granted which allowed Vanbrugh to build a private gallery pew for his friend and patron, John Holles, Duke of Newcastle. This is first referred to in Vanbrugh's letter to Brigadier Watkins, endorsed 'Nov. 1st 1723', a fact first noted by Professor Downes, in that Webb had to use the Coxe transcripts of the actual letters and had dated it '1716?'. A square brick addition to house the pew was made to the nave of Esher Old Church, and a separate entrance provided. Set a metre or so (4 ft) above the church floor, the elegant temple front faces into the church. Its columns are structural in that they support the joist and wall above. The pew was subsequently partitioned at its centre to also allow use by the Duke's brother.

87. KING'S WESTON, Gloucestershire. The South Front, 1712-4.

About 1710 Edward Southwell, a lawyer, asked Vanbrugh to design his house near Bristol. Whilst finished structurally by 1714, the interior remained incomplete at Southwell's death in 1730. The entrance front is dominated by six Corinthian pilasters paired at the ends and the more massive for being unfluted, and a crenellated arcade of chimney flues, a feature used on other occasions. The original south elevation had two Venetian windows, one above the other, in the centre bay. The mason was George Townesend, and the front was engraved in Colen Campbell's *Vitruvius Britannicus*, (1715) Vol. I, pl. 48.

88. KING'S WESTON, Gloucestershire. The Staircase, 1719-20, amended 1763-8.

The staircase remains basically as designed by Vanbrugh, but a glass roof was added later in the eighteenth century as part of Robert Mylne's internal alterations. Its form is a 'hanging staircase', that is without any inner supports. The niches contain painted urns and statues. On a grander scale Vanbrugh returned to the theme of grisaille painting in the niches of the Great Hall at Grimsthorpe, his last house (see **118, 120**).

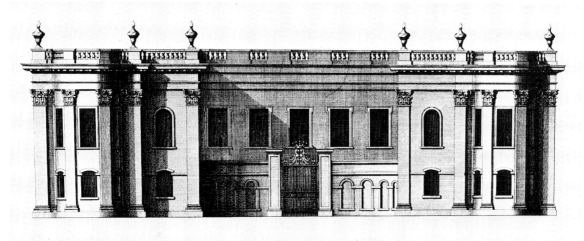

a Scale of 60 Feet

Extends 131

The North Prospect of Cholmondeley Hall in Cheshire The Seat of the R.t Hon.ble The Earl of Cholmondeley Treasurer of his Majesty's Houshold
to whom this Plate is most humbly Inscrib'd

Elevation Septentrionale de la Maison de Cholmondeley dans la Comte de Cheshire.

H Hulsbergh Sculp

89. KING'S WESTON, Gloucestershire. The East Front, 1712–14.

In the 1760s the architect Robert Mylne made alterations to Vanbrugh's work on the east and north fronts, as well as amending the interior. The 'frost-work' rusticated bands on the pilasters flanking the central open-pedimented window, and unusual emphasis to the window sills, does however still allow Vanbrugh's originality to dominate Mylne's amendments.

90. CHOLMONDELEY HALL, Cheshire. Project for the North Front, *c* 1713, Colen Campbell, *Vitruvius Britannicus*, II (1717) pl. 32 (Photograph: Birmingham Reference Library).

Cholmondeley Hall was partly remodelled by William Smith for the 1st Earl of Cholmondeley, 1704–13, but was demolished about 1805. It would seem that Smith, in effect, rebuilt the south end of the house. Vanbrugh wrote on 28 September 1713 that he had visited the house for a second time, and that he had prepared a scheme 'for what is left to do'. The north front is the one he referred to, but Vanbrugh's name is not mentioned by Campbell, and the proposal was not proceeded with.

91. KENSINGTON PALACE, The New Greenhouse, or the Orangery, South Front, 1704.

Whilst the Orangery is probably basically the work of Hawksmoor, research for the history of the King's Works established a letter from William Lowndes, Secretary to the Treasury. He wrote on 10 July 1704 to the Officers of the Works: 'I am commanded by the Lord Treasurer to acquaint you it is her Majesty's pleasure that the Green House at Kensington be made according to the alteration of the Draft proposed by Mr Vanbrugh.' The work was completed by the end of 1705, at a cost, which increased because of Vanbrugh's grander conception, from a little under £2600, to £6126.

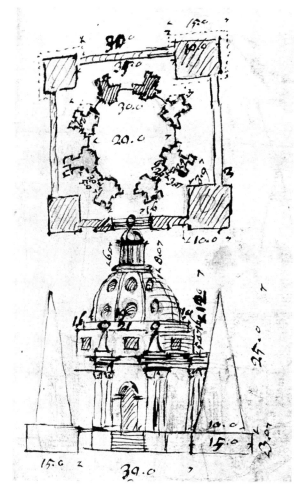

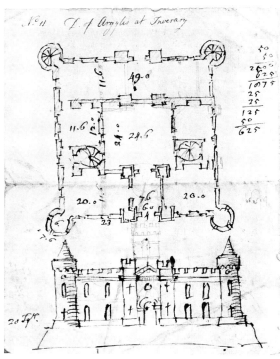

92. TEMPLE, Plan and Elevation of a circular Temple, with obelisks, *c* 1723? Pen and ink on paper, *William Proby Esq.* (Photograph: Courtauld Institute of Art).

This may have some connection with preliminary ideas for the Temple at Castle Howard. Vanbrugh refers to his work on plans for William Etty, and mentions its 'Porticos' and 'Obelisks' in letters on 1724–5. However the obelisk was a favourite Vanbrugh ornament and may have been intended for Claremont, or almost anywhere else he was working.

93. INVERARAY CASTLE, Argyll, Scotland. Sketch Plan and Elevation, pen and ink on paper, with pencil amendments, *c* 1720? inscr: 'No. 11 D. of Argyles at Inverary', *William Proby Esq.* (Photograph: Courtauld Institute of Art).

Vanbrugh's interest in the neo-medieval manner had already made itself manifest in his complex of buildings at Greenwich. This sketch for the 2nd Duke of Argyll represents a scheme which was not adopted, although Roger Morris attempted something similar in castellated Gothic for Inveraray, 1745-60. It is a small drawing which demonstrates the architect's spontaneity – of powerful castellation, with a pencil addition of a central tower, akin to the process of 'thinking out loud'.

143

94. SEVENOAKS, Kent. 'The Vine.' Elevation, *c* 1718, pen, ink and shaded wash on paper, *William Proby Esq.* (Photograph: Courtauld Institute of Art).
One of the designs by Vanbrugh for a small house for Colonel Lambert at Sevenoaks. The dimensions (at right) are incomplete, but suggest an overall height in the towers of about 8 metres (25 ft).

95-96. DESIGNS FOR SMALL HOUSES. Elevation and (**96**) Plan and Elevation, both pen, ink and wash on paper, *Victoria and Albert Museum, London*, No. D111-1891, and (**96**) No. D106-1891 (Photographs: Museum).
'The small house', one of Vanbrugh's most interesting design activities (discussed by Whistler, pp. 210-11, as 'The Little House on the Drawing-Board') has given plans and elevations of engaging whimsy. Few, if any, were built, but in the two shown here, that in **96** has only one bedroom and a small room on each side, all fitted with corridors, lobbies and an entrance hall with niches for statuary, put within overall dimensions of some 25 × 13 metres (82 × 41 ft). The plan resembles Vanbrugh's house of Chargate (see **84**) or that for Eastbury on a small scale (see **71**). Indeed there is a drawing for Eastbury on the back.

The elevation (**95**) has written on its back, seemingly by Vanbrugh: 'Coll. Lambert's house'. Colvin notes The Vine, Sevenoaks, Kent among Vanbrugh's 'doubtful and attributed works'. The house, now demolished, was, as this view shows, very simple in elevation.

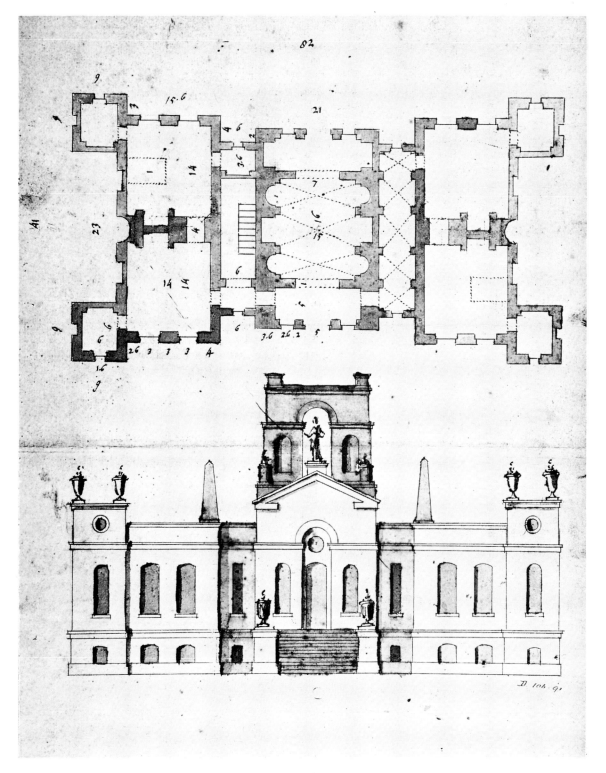

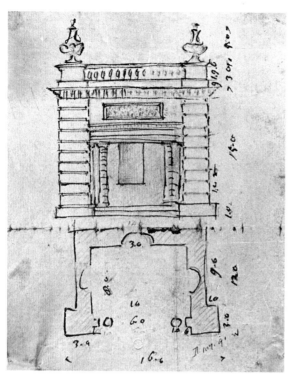

97. GARDEN SUMMER HOUSE, unidentified. Elevation and plan drawn by Vanbrugh, pen and ink on paper, *Victoria and Albert Museum, London*, No. D107-91 (Photograph: Courtauld Institute of Art).

An example of the massive effect which Vanbrugh could incorporate into a small building some 4 by 5 metres (13 × 16 ft) on plan, a little over 7 metres (23 ft) high to the top of the urns. The interior has three semi-circular niches, and a tablet for an inscription over the doorway. Vanbrugh wrote to the Duke of Newcastle in the autumn of 1719 that Dagley (a mason?) would see from a draft that 'the Tablet is design'd only to give the Middle break, a few shillings worth of distinction.' There is reason to think however he was not referring to this garden pavilion, but to Claremont.

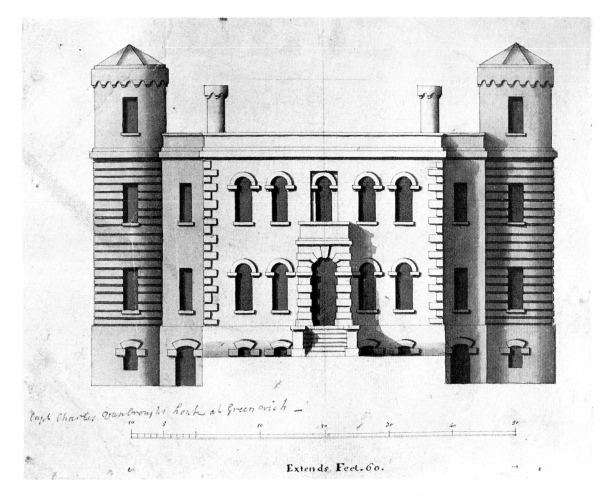

Capt Charles Vanbroughs house at Greenwich —

Extends Feet. 60.

98. WOLLATON HALL, Nottinghamshire. The South Front, 1580–8.

Among the outstanding architectural achievements of the Elizabethan age were the 'prodigy houses' – as Sir John Summerson has called them – and principally Wollaton, and Hardwick Hall, Derbyshire. With dramatic silhouette, and what Hawksmoor, in respect of Wollaton, called 'some true Stroakes of Architecture' they are the houses most likely to have impressed themselves on Vanbrugh's imagination by their spectacular all-round symmetry. He would pass near Hardwick when visiting Chatsworth, and could have seen Wollaton easily enough when travelling north, or when refitting the interior of nearby Nottingham Castle in 1719. His interest in medieval architecture, and preocupation with mass and 'movement' could all be given fanciful rein before houses which betokened such noble pasts, and expressed it all with gusto. Vanbrugh was to do something similar on at least one occasion – at Seaton Delaval.

99. GREENWICH, Vanbrugh House. Elevation, *c* 1721, pen, ink and shaded wash on paper, inscr: 'Capt Charles Vanbrough's house at Greenwich', *William Proby Esq.* (Photograph: Courtauld Institute of Art).

Vanbrugh established himself and various of his family in houses of his designing at Greenwich. Vanbrugh Castle was for the architect himself, 'The Nunnery' for a second brother, and Vanbrugh House or 'The Mince-Pie House' for his brother Charles. It was little more than 18 metres (53 ft) across and had stair-towers at the sides, and three ground-floor rooms (see **100**).

100. VANBRUGH CASTLE, Greenwich. The South Front, 1718-19.

The group of houses at Greenwich which were occupied by Vanbrugh and his family is discussed on p. 56. The architect had acquired a lease on land near the top of Greenwich Hill in 1718 – a year later he married Henrietta Yarburgh – and this may well have led him to build his castle, in all its asymmetrical complexity. From the Dover road across Blackheath the estate was approached through a brick archway (now gone). Down in the valley was Greenwich Hospital, still incomplete. Inside the house has 'most of the typical Vanbrugh features, but in little: vaulted corridors; stairs and closets in projecting towers; bow windows on every floor, allowing tribute to a fine view.'

101-102. STOWE HOUSE, Buckinghamshire. The North Portico, *c* 1720, with additions, finished 1772; and (**102**) in Jacques Rigaud and Bernard Baron's view from Sarah Bridgeman's *Views of Stowe* (1739) pl. 6.

On the north side Vanbrugh seems to have added the portico, but due to its similarity to the one Leoni designed for Lyme Hall, Cheshire it has been suggested he may have provided the Stowe feature, or worked out a sketch of Vanbrugh's. The front remained in this form for forty years with the corners raised as towers, and the dormers hidden by a balustrade. The north front appears like this in Charles Bridgeman's perspective view, and in Rigaud and Baron's view of 1739, illustrated here. In the 1760s Lord Temple seems to have got Georges François Blondel (who was altering Robert Adam's south front) to carry the attic up between the towers, and to add the colonnades.

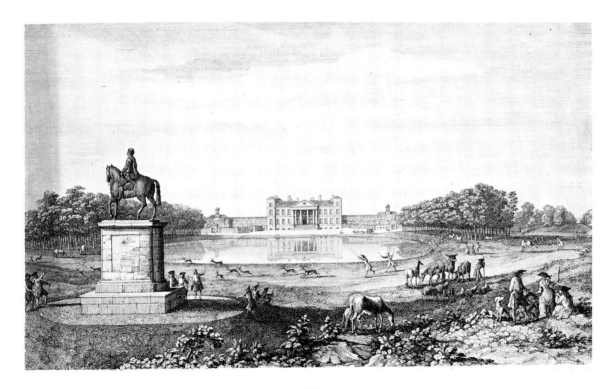

103. STOWE, Buckinghamshire. The Rotunda, 1733-4, by Jacques Rigaud, *Metropolitan Museum of Art, New York*, Harris Brisbane Dick Fund, 1942, No. 42.79(7) (Photograph: Museum).

The large group of engravings of Stowe by Rigaud (many reproduced by P. Willis, *Charles Bridgeman*, 1977) includes one which shows Vanbrugh's Rotunda, prior to its amendment by Borra in 1752. The temple 'was placed at a focal point of the old, half-geometrical gardens.' It had a dome supported on Roman Ionic capitals, and originally housed a gilt statue of Venus. There is a similar temple, presumably by Vanbrugh, at Duncombe Park, Yorkshire (*repr:* Downes, pl. 128).

104. HAMPTON COURT, Middlesex. Chimney-piece carved by Grinling Gibbons in the Queen's Presence Chamber.

A number of rooms in the east wing at Hampton Court were left incomplete at Queen Mary's death in 1694 and not finished until George I took up residence there. In July 1716 Vanbrugh visited the house with the Prince of Wales, who, with his wife and children was to use six of the rooms intended to be refurbished. The Queen's Guard Chamber, and the other rooms were given fine carved chimney-pieces (some in marble provided by the master mason, Benjamin Jackson) by Grinling Gibbons. He received £533 for his work which includes those in the presence chamber, and that showing a fine representation of the Royal Arms in the Music Room.

105. LUMLEY CASTLE, Durham. The West Front, begun 1722 (Photograph: National Monuments Record). On one of his northern journeys to Castle Howard in 1721 Vanbrugh travelled on to the far north to provide Lord Lumley with 'a General Design' for altering his medieval hill-top Castle. Inside Vanbrugh's work can now hardly be seen at all, and even outside his west front has 'little more than a good staircase and door, and some excellent sash and bull's-eye windows, introduced tact-fully into corner towers and the fronts between them.' But as Vanbrugh told Brigadier Watkins in his letter of 26 August 1721 'Lumley Castle is a Noble thing; and well deserves the Favours Lord Lumley designs to bestow upon it.' Richard Lumley succeeded his father as 2nd Earl of Scarbrough in 1721. The fine stuccoed interiors of the state rooms are of about 1730, but their sequence and size was presumably determined by Vanbrugh.

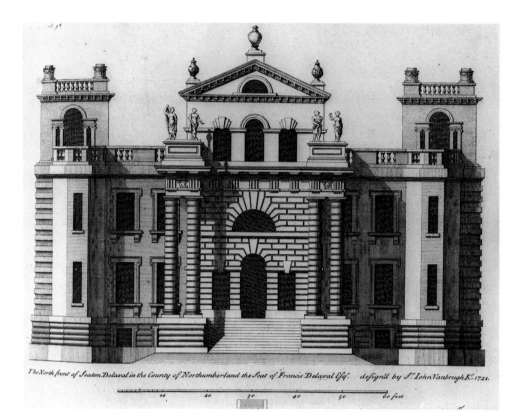

The North front of Seaton Delaval in the County of Northumberland the Seat of Francis Delaval Esq.   design'd by S.ʳ John Vanbrugh K.ᵗ 1721.

The South front of Seaton Delaval in the County of Northumberland the Seat of Francis Delaval Esq.   design'd by S.ʳ John Vanbrugh K.ᵗ 1721.

106–107. SEATON DELAVAL, Northumberland. Elevations of the North and South Fronts, 1721, Colen Campbell, *Vitruvius Britannicus*, III (1725) pls. 20, 21 (Photographs: Birmingham Reference Library).

These powerful compositions are perhaps slightly less imposing in actuality – unless the weather intervenes in a dramatic way on the exposed site – in that the two towers with Venetian windows are then viewed from an oblique angle. A number of embellishments such as urns and statues are also not present on the building itself. But the rhythm of the facades – although perhaps architecturally all wrong – still succeeds in a compelling way (see **106**).

108. SEATON DELAVAL, Northumberland. North Front, *c* 1722–4.

There is a spirited theatrical air – of the temporary arrest of dramatic movement – about the vast expanse of Seaton Delaval. Whilst the whole facade, with its east and west courts, spans over 130 metres, the centre block itself is small and concentrated. Six ringed Ionic columns in two groups of three punctuate the mass on this entrance side with calculated exaggeration, and are perhaps even more dominant in the *Vitruvius Britannicus* engraving, though only four are visible.

109. SEATON DELAVAL, Northumberland. Interior of the stables, East Wing, *c* 1724.

Sir John Summerson has written of Seaton Delaval itself that 'the different elements are worked together with a complete disregard for convention, and a magical eye for sheer effect.' This can also be seen within the various parts of the stable and kitchen courts – the swell of the ashlar stone partitions to the stalls, with their Baroque posts, the sweep of the arch springing from its stepped buttresses, the simple door surround – a blend of perspective, shadow and precisely cut stone. As Christopher Hussey wrote in his *Country Life* account in 1923 'None but princely chargers and the palfreys of potentates dare, surely, enter so august a stable?.'

110. SEATON DELAVAL, Northumberland. Staircase, West Wing, *c* 1724.

At either side of the Hall beneath the gallery there are vaulted passages which lead to the winding staircases. These are concealed within two heavily rusticated staircase towers which have four Venetian windows in the head of each. The staircases betoken Vanbrugh's involvement with the medieval, but there is, additionally, a fine Baroque touch about their spatial disposition, with the well-cut steps and the (now damaged) iron balustrading spiralling upwards.

154

111. SEATON DELAVAL, Northumberland. The Hall, *c* 1721.

The interior of the central block was destroyed by fire on 3 January 1822. In a later context the Carceri engravings of Piranesi come to mind, betokening high mysterious ruination. The six standing stucco figures in niches are probably the work of Giovanni Bagutti, who had worked at Castle Howard. They represent music, painting, sculp-ture, architecture, geography and astronomy and some are calcined to near destruction to show their metal armature and terracotta tile construction, and the hessian which was dipped in gypsum, and folded (to set) as simulated draperies. The chimneypiece is formed of two stucco torsos whch bear an entablature sculptured with a frieze of figures.

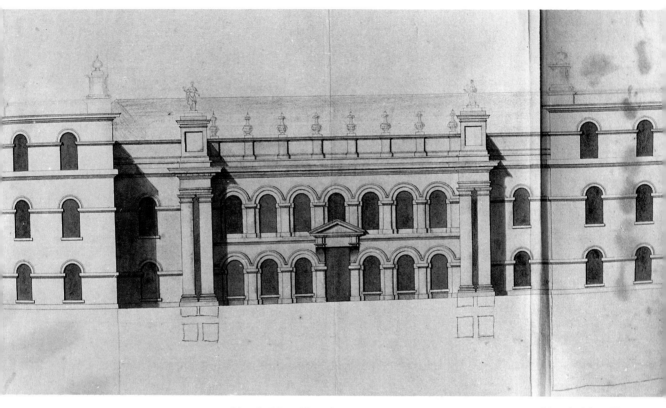

112. GRIMSTHORPE CASTLE, Lincolnshire. Elevation for North Front, c 1715, pen, ink, pencil, shaded wash on paper, *William Proby Esq.* (Photograph: Courtauld Institute of Art).

Grimsthorpe was Vanbrugh's last house. On 20 August 1723, he wrote to the Duke of Newcastle that he was to go forward with the design for the 1st Duke of Ancaster, by order of the 2nd Duke. He had worked in an unidentified capacity for the family in earlier years and this elevation differs from the final solution (see **115**), but the arcaded emphasis was still strong in the architect's mind.

113-114. GRIMSTHORPE CASTLE, Lincolnshire. Elevations of North and South Fronts, engraved in Colen Campbell, *Vitruvius Britannicus*, III (1725) pls. 12, 13 (Photographs: Birmingham Reference Library).

The engravings show the north entrance front, almost as built, for the 2nd Duke of Ancaster, and the proposed south garden front, which was not executed. The need to retain parts of the earlier house, was successfully hidden on the north side, but left exposed on the south.

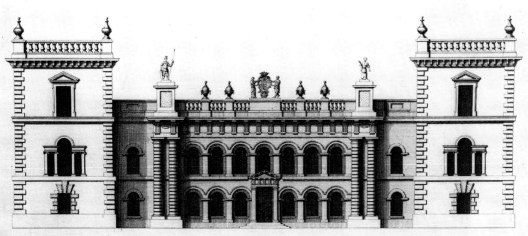

The North front of Grimsthorp in the County of Lincoln the Seat of his Grace the Duke of Ancaster and Kesteven Hereditary Lord great Chamberlain of England. Design'd by Sr. John Vanbrugh Kt. 1723.

Ca: Campbell delin:

H. Hulsbergh Sculp.

The Garden front of Grimsthorp in the County of Lincoln the Seat of his Grace the Duke of Ancaster and Kesteven Hereditary Lord great Chamberlain of England. Design'd by Sr. John Vanbrugh Kt. 1723.

C. Campbell delin.

H. Hulsbergh Sculp.

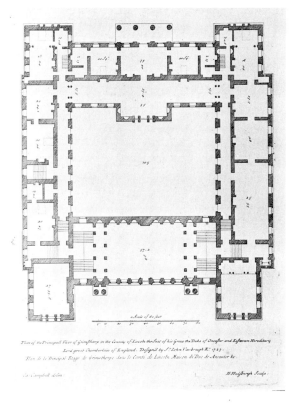

115. GRIMSTHORPE CASTLE, Lincolnshire. Plan of the principal floor, Colen Campbell, *Vitruvius Britannicus*, III (1725) pl. 11 (Photograph: Birmingham Reference Library).

Vanbrugh planned his last house in 1723 with medieval Lumley Castle still in his mind. The old house was to be set within four corner towers and between those on the east and west corners (bottom of the illustration) he would place the entrance hall with its double-arcaded screens and half-revealed staircases (see **118**). A gallery was planned, running around the house, with the state rooms leading off, and with windows looking out into the central courtyard. But, alas, only the northern range and its entrance front was carried out before the architect's death in 1726.

116. GRIMSTHORPE CASTLE, Lincolnshire. The North Front, 1715–30 (?).

We have already commented on the differences between this majestic north front and the other elevations. The plan and elevations were published in the third volume of Colen Campbell's *Vitruvius Britannicus* (1725) (see **113–115**). In the rustication there are references to Seaton Delaval and Lumley Castle, particularly the use of four towers and the forecourt with blank arcaded walls. The hall front between the towers was amended from an earlier drawing (see **112**) to give the magnificent paired Doric columns a banded treatment. There is a mighty entablature, and balustrade, with parapet, urns, and (at the centre, the Bertie arms). The pedimented doorway with its columns is a late variant, perhaps after Vanbrugh's death, from the one on brackets he envisaged.

The low walls to east and west have 26 bays of rusticated niches, linked to the two-storey pavilions. Connecting them is the iron grille and gates upon which a local smith, probably from Stamford, was working *c* 1730. Edward Nutt, noted as the smith in the Pevsner, 'Buildings of England', *Lincolnshire* volume (1964, p. 555) was in fact a mason, as the Grimsthorpe archives (Lincolnshire County Record Office) make clear.

117. GRIMSTHORPE CASTLE, Lincolnshire. The West Front, left, 1723–6; right, 1811.

This view shows how, at Vanbrugh's death, he had added the north front (with the north-west corner tower of three bays which houses the Chapel, shown here) but had done little to advance the west front. His tower abuts a bay window from the time when Charles Brandon, Duke of Suffolk (who had married the 10th Lord Willoughby's daughter) enlarged the castle shortly before 1541, when Henry VIII paid a visit. This bay is at the position of one of the four thirteenth-century corner towers built in the castle of Gilbert de Gant. That at the south-east corner, called 'King John's Tower' survives, but in a form modified by the Tudor rebuilding. In 1811 Vanbrugh's partly built west wing was demolished, a new Tudor-style front with narrow chimneystacks was built to the designs of Henry Garling and Samuel Page, working for Lord Gwydir.

118. GRIMSTHORPE CASTLE, Lincolnshire. The Great Hall, looking west.

The Great Hall 12 × 33 metres (40 × 110 ft) is Vanbrugh's finest room at Grimsthorpe, and, arguably, in any of his houses. The two-storey arcading of the north front is continued inside with the blind arcades containing grisaille paintings of English Kings by Sir James Thornhill. This view shows four of the seven, George I, William III, Henry VIII, and Henry VII (the other three being William I, Edward III and Henry V). The ceiling, with its concave oval centre (perhaps intended for painting) has its pattern repeated in the black and cream pattern of the floor. Willoughby heads flank the chimney entablature which is surmounted by a ducal coronet over a monogrammed shield. Cartouches of cherubs' heads supporting festoons and ducal coronets can be seen to the left and right of the arcade.

119. GRIMSTHORPE CASTLE, Lincolnshire. The East Entrance Hall, *c* 1723.
Leaving the Great Hall through the vaulted aisle of the arcade is the East Entrance Hall, which had acted as the Servants' Hall. This is set under the State Dining Room which is on the first floor of the north-east tower. With its tripartite vaulting it is similar to the under croft at Lumley Castle and is an impressive indication of the mason's craft.

120–121. GRIMSTHORPE CASTLE, Lincolnshire. The Great Hall, looking east, and (**121**) the staircase and doorway to the East Wing.

For a note on the Great Hall see that to **118**. The lower stage of the open arcade leads to a superbly balustraded two-flighted staicase, which is also repeated at the west end of the Hall (see **118**). The ironwork is now attributed to Thomas Warren (d. 1736) who worked for Vanbrugh at Blenheim, and (probably) at Kimbolton. The central pedimented doorway has a casing which may have been designed by Hawksmoor. According to Professor Downes its form derives from those designed by Michelangelo for the side palaces of the Capitol in Rome.

122. CHATHAM, Kent. Main Gate to the Dockyard, *c* 1720.

There is, as noted, no direct evidence that either Vanbrugh or Hawksmoor were involved in the design of buildings for the Board of Ordnance. However the mass of documentation may still yield clues. For the moment the position is as summarised by Whistler (pp. 212–226), and Downes (p. 124); that is that Vanbrugh *may* have been the designing hand, with the various craftsmen carrying out the work under the supervision of the Board's district engineers. The Chatham gateway is more or less a larger version of that to Vanbrugh Fields, Greenwich (Downes, pl. 104, now demolished).

123. CHATHAM, Kent. The Great Storehouse. Begun 1717 (Photograph provided by Laurence Whistler).

A contemporary elevation and plan of the Great Storehouse at Chatham is inscribed 'begun in the Year. 1717'. Laurence Whistler, who has made a serious attempt to chart the vagaries of 'Ordnance Vanbrugh' suggests that Vanbrugh and Hawksmoor may have submitted designs but not have played any part in the actual erection of such buildings 'for which the usual servants of the Board were adequate'. Andrews Jelfe, a master mason (who was in partnership with Christoper Cass – the mason Vanbrugh recommended to complete Blenheim) did work for the Board of Ordnance, and may be the executant, if not the author.

124. ROYAL ARSENAL, Woolwich, Board Room and Saloon, *c* 1717. View by Paul Sandby, 1779 (Photograph provided by Laurence Whistler Esq.).

Woolwich had been a depot of the Ordnance from the time of Henry VIII, settling on a new site at Tower Place at 1671. The sixteenth-century house became the residence of the Lieutenant-General of Ordnance. The Royal Laboratory was transferred to the site in 1695, and in 1717 the Government set up its own brass foundry for the casting of guns. Whilst the buildings of 1717 are in what we call the 'Ordnance Vanbrugh' style there is no direct evidence to connect him. The tower of Tower Place can be seen in Sandby's view: one would like to think that its survival when the house was pulled down was due to Vanbrugh's appreciation of its qualities, an

extension of his concern to save Woodstock Manor (see **38**). But this is fanciful, and the tower finally went in 1786 leaving the 'powerful, even bleak elevation' with its large arch, supporting a gable treated as an open pediment, with a lion and unicorn on plinths either side of the door. At the north end a bow window faces the river just visible at the right of Sandby's view. He has indicated a sail-masted vessel on the river itself. The interior has a hall with a large room at each side, in which are massive fireplaces. The room on the left was used after 1741 by the Royal Military Academy. For the present state of the building, see the description by Bridget Cherry and Nikolaus Pevsner, *Buildings of England, London 2: South* (1983) pp. 286-9.

125. SIR JOHN VANBRUGH (1664-1726). Painting by Jonathan Richardson, oil on canvas, 104.8 × 89.2 cm (41¼ × 33⅛ in), *The Corporation of Queen's Heralds and Pursuivants of Arms* (Photograph: A. C. Cooper).
This three-quarter length of Vanbrugh depicts him in a red watered silk robe and the badge of Clarenceux Herald, holding a plan inscribed *Blenheim* in his left hand. It was engraved with slight variations by Faber in 1727 and stated on the plate to have been painted by Richardson in 1725, the year before Vanbrugh's death. The portrait was purchased by the College of Arms in 1824 (see also frontispiece, and **1**).

NOTES TO THE ILLUSTRATIONS

1 David Piper, *Catalogue of the seventeenth-century portraits in the National Portrait Gallery, 1625–1714* (1963), p. 357; Downes, pp. 98–9.

3 Whistler, pp. 197–9.

4 Colvin and Craig, No. 112.

8 Webb, *Letters*, pp. 163–4; Whistler, pp. 60–1.

9 Webb, *Letters*, p. 162; Whistler, pp. 60–1, pls. 7, 16.

10 Whistler, p. 41, Pl. 11; Downes, p. 30, Pls. 18–21.

11 K. Downes, *English Baroque Architecture* (1966), pls. 229–230.

13-14 Whistler, Pls. 4–5; Downes, pp. 32–3.

15 *Wren Soc.* XII, pl. XL; XVII pl. XIII; Whistler, p. 35, pl. 1; Downes, p. 29, pl. 18.

17 Whistler, p. 45, pl. 12.

20 M. Whinney and O. Millar, *English Art, 1625–1714* (1957) pp. 222, fn 3, 336.

21 Freidrich Walter, *Das Mannheimer Schloss* (Karlsruhe, 1927); M. Whinney and O. Millar, *English Art, 1625–1714* (1957) p. 336, fn 2.

22 Downes, p. 23.

28 Whistler, pp. 69–70.

29 Whistler, p. 59, pls. 9–10.

30 Christopher Hussey, *English Gardens and Landscapes, 1700–1750*, (1967), Ch. XIV.

31 Whistler, pp. 74–5; Downes, p. 109.

35 Green, *Blenheim*, pp. 183, 186, 243, 318; John Harris, *Sir William Chambers* (1970) p. 199.

36 Green, *Sarah, Duchess of Marlborough* (1967), following p. 128.

37 Green, *Blenheim*, pp. 298–9.

38 Webb, *Letters*, p. 29, 'Reasons Offere'd for Preserving some Part of the Old Manor'; Green, *Blenheim*, pp. 31, 42.

39 Green, *Blenheim*, pls. 25, 32.

42 David Green, *Gardener to Queen Anne: Henry Wise, 1653–1738, and the Formal Garden* (1956); Green, *Blenheim*, p. 68; Peter Willis, *Charles Bridgeman* (1977) p. 46.

44 Downes, p. 247.

45 Anthony Blunt, *Art and Architecture in France, 1500–1700*, 2nd edn., revd., (1973) pp. 236, 425 fns 50, 51; R. W. Berger, *Antoine Le Pautre* (New York, 1969).

54 Green, *Blenheim*, p. 84.

55-56 Green, *Blenheim*, p. 249; Downes, pp. 66–7.

59 Colvin and Craig, No. 232V.

60 Green, *Blenheim*, pp. 306–7; Whistler, p. 104.

61 Green, *Blenheim*, pp. 123–4; Whistler, pp. 106–7.

62 Webb, *Letters*, p. 89; Green, *Blenheim*, pp. 306–8.

64 Green, *Blenheim*, pp. 63, 146; Whistler, pp. 101, 104–6.

65 Colvin and Craig, No. 233.

66 Downes, p. 255, pl. 74.

67 Green, *Blenheim*, pp. 26, 125, 230, 312; Downes, p. 73.

69 Whistler, pp. 157–8, pls. 61–2.

70 Whistler, pp. 156–9, pls. 60–7; Downes, pp. 114–118, pls. 133–9.

71 Downes, p. 117.

76-79 Whistler, pp. 172-7; Downes, p. 117; John Harris, *The Artist and the Country House* (1979) pls. 214a, & b.

80 Whistler, pp. 130-40, pl. 51.

82 Webb, *Letters*, pp. 24-5; Paul Drury, 'The evolution of Audley End, 1605-1745', *Architectural History*, Vol. 23 (1980) pp. 3-39. Drury's paper amends the conclusions set out by Nikolaus Pevsner, 'Good King James's Gothic', *Architectural Review*, CVII (1950) pp. 117-22.

84 Tipping and Hussey, pp. 167-74; Whistler, pls. 57-8; Downes, pp. 51-2, 100.

85 Downes, pls. 115-116 (showing condition in 1962 and 1976).

86 Webb, *Letters*, p. 83; Downes, pp. 80 fn 9, 118.

87 Webb, *Letters*, p. 80; Kerry Downes, ed., 'The King's Weston Book of Drawings', *Architectural History*, X (1967) pp. 9-88, figs. 7, 8.

89 C. Gotch, 'Mylne at King's Weston', *Country Life*, January 23, 1953, pp. 212-15.

90 Colvin, *Dictionary*, p. 750; Downes, p. 92 fn 41.

91 Colvin, *King's Works*, V (1976) pp. 193-4.

92 Webb, *Letters*, pp. 157, 8, 9, 160; Colvin and Craig, No. 148.

93 Ian G. Lindsay and Mary Cosh, *Inveraray and the Dukes of Argyll* (1973); Colvin and Craig, No. 79.

94 Colvin and Craig, No. 159; Colvin, *Dictionary*, p. 854.

95-96 Colvin and Craig, 23-4; Colvin, *Dictionary*, p. 854.

97 Webb, *Letters*, p. 119.

98 Downes, p. 54.

99 Whistler, pls. 88-9; Colvin and Craig, No. 167; Downes, pp. 96-7, pls. 108-9.

100 Whistler, pp. 202-3; K. Downes in *Country Life*, 159, May 27, 1976, pp. 1406-8.

101-102 *Country Life*, February 19, 1959; G. B. Clarke in *Stoic* [Stowe School magazine], XXIII, July 1969, pp. 257-64; P. Willis, *Charles Bridgeman* (1977) Ch. 5.

104 Colvin, *King's Works*, V (1976) pp. 176-8.

105 Webb, *Letters*, p. 138; Whistler, p. 17; Downes, p. 106.

107 Whistler, p. 18, pls. 134-5.

112 Webb, *Letters*, p. 151; Colvin and Craig, No. 162; Downes, p. 119, pl. 156.

113-114 Tipping and Hussey, pp. 298-300; H. M. Colvin, 'Grimsthorpe Castle, The North Front', in *The Country Seat*, ed., H. M. Colvin and J. Harris (1970); Downes, pl. 153.

115 Whistler, p. 17.

118 Downes, p. 121.

119 Tipping and Hussey, pl. 435, 457.

120-121 Downes, p. 121.

123 Whistler, pp. 214-5.

APPENDIXES

A: VANBRUGH'S LETTERS

In 1927–8 the Nonesuch Press edition of *The Complete Works of Sir John Vanbrugh* appeared in four volumes, of which the first three contained the plays, edited by Bonamy Dobrée, and the fourth, Geoffrey Webb's edition of the *Letters*. Professor Webb explained in his preface that 'the letters to the Duke and Duchess of Marlborough and some others connected with the building of Blenheim Palace' could only be reproduced from Archdeacon Coxe's transcripts in the British Museum. He had not been allowed to consult the originals. Nevertheless his edition has stood the test of time well, although some amendments to text and dating have ensued over the years (see *Bibliography: Manuscripts* for details of the transfer of items from Blenheim to the British Library.) The deposit may contain two or three letters which are not in the Downes list, but which relate to Blenheim, (e.g. one of the two letters to Lord Godolphin, 1709, (Webb, *Letters*, p. 27, gives that of 31 May 1709); and that of 1722 to Henrietta, 2nd DS of M, Countess of Godolphin, MS 61432, f.128).

In 1954 Laurence Whistler included in his *The Imagination of Vanbrugh* 25 letters not in Webb. A list of all the letters known up to 1977 formed a valuable appendix (K) in Professor Kerry Downes's *Vanbrugh* (1977). Since that date the following have been published, or noted.

The letter of 20 September 1721, noted by Downes appeared in part in Bernard Harris's *Sir John Vanbrugh* (British Council, 1967, 'Writers and their Work', No. 197, p. 15) An unsigned letter, seemingly by Vanbrugh, dated 16 August 1722, forms part of instructions to George Cansfield about the round window at Seaton Delaval. This document is displayed at the house, and is reproduced, with a transcript, in Madeleine M. Bingham's *Masks and Facades: Sir John Vanbrugh, the Man in his Setting* (1974). It is convenient to list the published sources of some other newly discovered documents and letters, even if listed by Downes. Note should be taken of:

R. Kern, 'Documents relating to Theatre Management', *Theatre Notebook*, XIV (1959)

John Barnard, 'Sir John Vanbrugh: Two unpublished letters', *Huntington Library Quarterly*, XXIX (1966) pp. 347–52

Albert Rosenberg, 'New Light on Vanbrugh' (eight letters), *Philological Quarterly*, XLV (1966) pp. 606–13

A. R. Huseboe, 'Additions to Vanbrugh's Correspondence', *Philological Quarterly*, LIII (1974)

Ragnhild Hatton, *George I, Elector and King* (1978) p. 147, letter of November 23, 1715, in Görtz archives, Darmstadt

Juliet Milhous, 'Five New Letters from Vanbrugh' (at Harvard and Princeton; relate to work at Blenheim, and as a Herald) *Harvard Library Bulletin*, 27 (1979) pp. 434–42

Kerry Downes, 'Vanbrugh's Heslington's lady': undated letter (1717) to the Duke of Newcastle (British Library, Add MS., 32686 ff. 104–5), *The Burlington Magazine* 124 (March 1982) pp. 153–5.

Letters which are published at future dates (Milhous notes some in her 1979 article), are usually traced by the annual abstracting publications cited in my *Bibliography: Drama*. The changed location of some items, from Blenheim to the British Library, is also noted therein: *Manuscript Sources*.

B: VANBRUGH AND THE BOARD OF ORDNANCE

In *Architectural Review*, December 1952, and in his *The Imagination of Vanbrugh* (1954) pp. 213–226, Laurence Whistler drew attention to various naval and military buildings 'on the edge of the Thames at Woolwich, at Berwick-on-Tweed, and in several famous dockyard towns'. They were in 'the Vanbrugh–Hawksmoor manner' and he described them under the appellation 'Ordnance-Vanbrugh'. They were all built between 1716 and 1721. Downes notes (p. 124) 'Whether Vanbrugh designed any of them personally cannot be established, and there are certainly different degrees of closeness to his personal style.' It is not even easy to list the buildings (below) as many are gone, altered, or formed part of a complex which was subsequently rebuilt.

Woolwich, Royal Arsenal The Royal Brass Foundry; the River Gate; Old Royal Military Academy (**124**); Grand (now Dial) Square; Sea and Land Carriage Houses; Board Room and Saloon (see Bridget Cherry and Nickolaus Pevsner, *The Buildings of England, London 2: South* (1983) pp. 286–8).

Chatham, Royal Naval Dockyard Main Gate (**122**); Great (Grand) Storehouse (**123**).

Portsmouth Her Majesty's Dockyard. The Landport Gate; the Carriage House; Grand Storehouse (?); Gunners' Barracks on Gun Wharfe; Officers' Barracks. (Only the Landport Gate survives, Whistler p. 222, and pl. 108).

Plymouth (Devonport) Gun Wharf (Downes pls. 144, 146); two Roperies (?).

Berwick-on-Tweed Entrance Gate; Barracks (two blocks 1717, after 1725) (Whistler, pls. 114–15).

The work of the Ordnance has been examined by Nigel P. Barker in a 1986 Reading University Ph.D Thesis, *The Architecture of the British Board of Ordnance, 1660–1750*. This has been prepared under the supervision of Professor K. Downes, who is also (1986) preparing a biography of Vanbrugh.

BIBLIOGRAPHICAL
NOTES

The following lists are selective, and reference is made to various annual abstracts in respect of the literary work. References in my chapter and illustration notes, together with those of a similar nature in Whistler (1954), Downes (1977) and Colvin, *Dictionary* (1978), should supply the reader with most of what he needs, other than the greater enjoyment of visiting Vanbrugh houses. Caution should be exercised at Laurence Whistler's article 'Vanbrugh Wemyss', *Country Life*, June 10, 1971. It was intended for the issue of April 1st.

(1) *Manuscripts (Blenheim)*
As several documents, letters, etc., relating to Vanbrugh's work at Blenheim have been transferred, in lieu of duty, to the British Library since Downes, (1977) was published, a list is given below, with the Additional Manuscripts' call numbers. References in sources such as David Green, *Blenheim Palace* (1951) to their location at the house need revision in view of this circumstance. A full calendar is in process by the British Library (1985).

Abbreviations:	D. of M.	1st Duke of Marlborough
(used in the first	DS of M.	Sarah, 1st Duchess of
section only)		Marlborough
	N. H.	Nicholas Hawksmoor
	J. V.	Sir John Vanbrugh

Agreement on behalf of D. of M. with Sir Thos. Wheate, 1705. Copy. 61353, f. 1.

Contract, erection of lime-kilns, Woodstock, 1705, 61354, f. 97.

Correspondence with D. of M./DS of M., 1705–17 (Partly copies). 61353, ff. 3–234; 61655, f. 35.

Reports of J.V., as Clarenceux Herald, 1707–17. 61540, f. 35; 61638, f. 77; 61649, f. 124.

J.V., letters to Lord Sunderland, 1707, 61605, ff. 179–182b; 1718, 61619, ff. 107–109 (Whistler, p. 244).

J.V., Memoranda relating to building at Blenheim, 1708–*c* 1721, (partly autograph). 61172, f. 219; 61353, ff. 70, 71b, 135–136b, 153–155b, 224–227; 61345, ff. 6–18, 22, 28, 29b, 32–33b; 61356, f. 33.

J.V., Letter to Lord Godolphin, 1709, 61353, f. 52.

Memorandum relating to Manor House, Woodstock, 1709
   (Autograph, and copies) 61353, ff. 62–67b.
Letter to 2nd Earl of Godolphin, 1709, 61353, f. 72.
Letter to T. Hopkins, 1709 (Whistler, p. 233) 61523, f. 244.
Papers relating to Blenheim law-suits, 1709–1720s, 61356, *passim.*
J.V., A letter to, 1710, 61353, f. 123.
   Letter to S. Travers, 1710, (Webb, *Letters*, p. 38), 61353, f. 133.
Correspondence with the Treasury, 1710–1716? (partly copies), 61353, ff. 121, 151; 61356, ff. 37–40b, 53–54b; 109–111b.
J.V., Memorandum relating to expenses and salary, 1711, 61353, f. 137.
Agreement on Behalf of D. of M. with G. Lowe, before 1715 (copy), (see Green, *Blenheim*, p. 135), 61354, ff. 122b–123.
Correspondence with T. Bobart, 1716 (partly copies), 61353, ff. 220–223b; (annotated in 1716), 61354, f. 40.
J.V., Letter to Duke of Newcastle, 1719 (Whistler, p. 244), 61605, ff. 185–188b.
J.V., Letter to Henrietta (2nd Duchess of Marlborough), Countess of Godolphin, 1722, 61432, f. 128.
J.V., Letter to W. Guidott, 1724 (Whistler, p. 245), (copy), 61353, f. 250.
T. Bobart, 'Not done' plan (Green, *Blenheim*, pl. 68), 1710, further stages, 1712–16, 61355, Vol. CCLV, ff. 18.
Blenheim Papers, Correspondence etc., Vols. CCLIII–CCLVII, 1705–42, 61353–57.
Blenheim, Chronology of Work, 1707–37, 61354, f. 115.
Purchase of statues (Green, *Blenheim*, p. 110), 61253, ff. 244–251.
Management, Park and Borough, 1710–41, 61468.
Removal of D. of M.'s body from
   (a) Windsor Lodge to London, 61410
   (b) to Blenheim Chapel, 1744, 61409, ff. 20–22b.
Accounts of monies expended by D. of M., 1681–1716, 19591–19618; 61347.

N.H., Contract witnessed by, 1705, 61354, f. 97.
  Treasury payments to, 1708-12, 61356, f. 53.
  Estimates, 1714, 61354, ff. 28-29b.
  Letters to DS of M., 1722-5, (Green, *Blenheim*, pp. 310-11), 61353, ff. 240, 252-255b.

(2) *Manuscripts, Borthwick Institute of Historical Research, York.*
The deposit of Vanbrugh-Yarburgh papers has been well used by Downes (1977), including an edition therein (pp. 180-241) of Sir John Vanbrugh's manuscript journal, 1715-26 (see **5**).

(3) *Literary Works*
There is a steady outpouring of articles on J.V.'s literary work. These are listed in the *Annual Bibliography of English Language and Literature* (Modern Humanities Research Association); *The Year's Work in English Studies*; and *The Scriblerian.*

A useful quick summary of some Vanbrugh titles published prior to 1967 is in Bernard Harris, *Sir John Vanbrugh*, British Council: Writers and their Work No. 197 (1967). The bibliographical side is treated in more detail by S. Wells, ed., *English Drama (excluding Shakespeare): Select Bibliographical Guides* (1975), notes on 'Vanbrugh', by John Barnard. Among many articles mention might be made of:

P. Meuschke and J. Fleisher, 'A Re-evaluation of Vanbrugh', *Publications, Modern Language Association*, XLIX (1934)

S. J. Rogal, 'John Vanbrugh and the Blenheim Palace controversy', *Journal, Society of Architectural Historians*, 33 (December 1974) pp. 293-303, deals with the waste of the building at Blenheim from the literary scholar's viewpoint.

Three American theses are relevant:

G. M. Berkowitz, 'The plays of Sir John Vanbrugh, and the comedy of the late seventeenth century', University of Indiana (1969): *Dissertation Abstracts* 30, 2997A.

D. L. Greene, 'Sir John Vanbrugh: a study of his comedies'. Univ. of Pennsylvania (1976): *Dissertation Abstracts* 36, 311-12A.

F. G. McCormick, 'The embattled career of Sir John Vanbrugh'. University of Minnesota (1977): *Dissertation Abstracts* 39, 901A.

Books and articles on the London stage, and on Vanbrugh's theatrical activities are also numerous. See, in particular, W. B. van Lennep, *The London Stage, 1600-1800*, 2 vols., Southern Illinois Univ. Press (1960) and:

R. Kern, 'Documents relating to Theatre Management', *Theatre Notebook*, XIV (1959)

Donald C. Mullin, 'The Queen's Theatre Haymarket: Vanbrugh's Opera House', *Theatre Survey*, VI (Nov. 1967) pp. 84-105

Philip Olleson, 'Vanbrugh and Opera at the Queen's Theatre, Haymarket', *Theatre Notebook*, 26 (1972) pp. 94-101

for details of the Collier attack in 1698, see the article by A. Williams, *Publications, Modern Language Association*, 90 (1975) pp. 234-46

Judith Milhous, New Light on Vanbrugh's Haymarket Theatre project, *Theatre Studies*, 17 (1977) pp. 143-161; her book, *Thomas Betterton and the management of Lincoln's Inn Fields, 1695-1709*, Southern Illinois University Press (1979) is invaluable for summarising recent research (see her article noted here in Appendix A: Letters).

Apart from Dobrée's edition of all the plays, the editions of *The Relapse* and *The Provok'd Wife* (both 1970, ed., Curt A. Zimansky) are recommended.

(4) *Biographical Studies*
As editor of the plays (1927-8) Bonamy Dobrée had a wide knowledge of Vanbrugh. Apart from his introduction to the Nonesuch Press edition, he wrote about Vanbrugh in his *Restoration Comedy* (1924), and his *Essays in Biography* (1925). The superbly written life by Laurence Whistler, *Sir John Vanbrugh: Architect and Dramatist* (1938), has not been superseded, except in some small points of detail, occasioned by more recent discoveries, many made by the author himself. I have referred in my chapter notes to articles by Paul Hopkins, F. G. McCormick on Vanbrugh's imprisonment in France, and on his part in the attack on Brest in 1694 by R. J. Jordan.

(5) *Architecture*
The introduction by Geoffrey Webb to his edition of the *Letters*, Vol. IV (1928) of the Nonesuch Press publication has endured as a perceptive study. It was followed, also in 1928, by H. Avray Tipping and Christopher Hussey's well-illustrated folio in the English Homes series (Vol. IV, pt. 2), *The Work of Sir John Vanbrugh and his School, 1699-1736*. These two statements rendered it unnecessary to consult with any frequency (for architectural detail) the earlier biographical studies by M. Dametz, *John Vanbrugh's Leben und Werke* (Vienna, 1898) and Christian Barman, *Sir John Vanbrugh* (1924).

The two well-documented studies, with full bibliographical references, are Laurence Whistler, *The Imagination of Vanbrugh and his Fellow Artists* (1954) and Kerry Downes, *Vanbrugh* (1977). Vanbrugh's associations with the King's Works are dealt with by H. M. Colvin, ed., *The History of the King's Works*, Vol V, 1660-1782 (1976). Accurate lists of Vanbrugh's buildings are in Downes (1977), and H. M. Colvin, *A Biographical Dictionary of British Architects, 1600-1840* (1978). Madeleine E.

Bingham's *Masks and Facades: Sir John Vanbrugh, the man in his setting* (1974) is adequate for a reader who does not want a detailed and foot-noted discussion of the architectural work.

Vanbrugh's drawings, many of which are illustrated by Whistler (1954), Downes (1977) and in this present study, are also discussed in H. M. Colvin and M. Craig, *Architectural Drawings in the Library at Elton Hall by Sir John Vanbrugh...*; that is, the collection of Sir Richard Proby, Bt. (Roxburghe Club, 1964).

Vanbrugh's fruitful association with Nicholas Hawksmoor is treated sympathetically by Kerry Downes, *Hawksmoor*, 2nd ed. (1969).

Vanbrugh's great house of Blenheim is carefully examined by David Green, *Blenheim Palace* (1951); and James Lees-Milne, *English Country Houses: Baroque* (1970), apart from chapters in Whistler, and Downes. See also Maynard Mack, 'Vanbrugh to Marlborough', *Scriblerian*, 9 (1977) pp. 77–83. One recent discovery arising from the deposit of Blenheim papers at the British Library is a Baroque design (Add MS. 61244, f. 150), for the Grand Cabinet, by Peter Strudel (1660–1714). This is discussed by Peter Draper, *Journal, Warburg and Courtauld Institutes*, 47 (1984) pp. 119-135.

(6) *Gardening*
We are in need of a thorough study of the relationship of English and French gardening theory to Vanbrugh's work. A number of studies at the edge are, however, most valuable. They are listed by Morris R. Brownell, 'Bursting Prospect: British Garden History Now' in R. P. Maccubbin and Peter Martin, eds., *British and American Gardens in the Eighteenth Century*, The Colonial Williamsburg Foundation, (1984) pp. 5–18. A useful selection to start with would be Christopher Hussey, *English Gardens and Landscape, 1700-1750* (1967); Joseph Burke, *English Art, 1714-1800* (1976) chapter 2, pp. 39–68; Peter Willis, *Charles Bridgeman and the English Landscape Garden* (1977); David Green, *Henry Wise, Gardener to Queen Anne* (1956); and Dora Wiebenson, *The Picturesque Garden in France*, Princeton (1978).

The theatre's relation to garden design – of great potential importance for Vanbrugh studies – has been explored, in part, by Susan Lang, 'The Genesis of the English Landscape Garden', in Nikolaus Pevsner, ed., *The Picturesque Garden and its Influence Outside the British Isles*, Dumbarton Oaks, Washington D.C. (1974), and by J. Dixon Hunt, in *The Figure in the Landscape: Poetry, Painting and Gardening during the Eighteenth Century*, Baltimore, (1976); in his essay in Inga-Stina Ewbank, ed., *Essays and Studies* (1980); and in his Franklin Jasper Walls Lectures at the Pierpont Morgan Library, New York (1981, to be published).

The important garden at Stowe is dealt with in a chapter in Willis, *op. cit.*, and by George Clarke and M.J. Gibbon, in Stowe School's magazine, *The Stoic*, XXIV (December 1969), XXIV (July 1970), and in their articles in a special number of *Apollo*, XCVII (June 1973). See also Morris R. Brownell, *Alexander Pope and the Arts of Georgian England* (1978), and Peter Martin, 'Pursuing Innocent Pleasures': The Gardening World of Alexander Pope, Hamden, Conn. (1983) for discussion of his most important influence in the Vanbrugh years. Pope's Timon's villa in the *Epistle to Burlington* has been thought to be the fictional counterpart of Houghton, or Blenheim (in Brownell, *op. cit.*), and most recently, Chatsworth. Peter Smithers's *Life of Addison* (1978) is referred to here in chapter I, p. 11. Whilst noted here as the last reference Addison may be among the first and most important influences on Vanbrugh's gardening ideas.

INDEX

Figures in **bold** refer to illustrations.